Good Girls,
Bad Girls

Good Girls, Bad Girls

The Enduring Lessons
of Twelve Women
of the Old Testament

T. J. Wray

ROWMAN & LITTLEFIELD PUBLISHERS, INC.
Lanham • Boulder • New York • Toronto • Plymouth, UK

ROWMAN & LITTLEFIELD PUBLISHERS, INC.

Published in the United States of America
by Rowman & Littlefield Publishers, Inc.
A wholly owned subsidary of The Rowman & Littlefield Publishing Group, Inc.
4501 Forbes Boulevard, Suite 200, Lanham, Maryland 20706
www.rowmanlittlefield.com

Estover Road
Plymouth PL6 7PY
United Kingdom

Distributed by National Book Network

British Library Cataloguing in Publication Information Available

Library of Congress Cataloging-in-Publication Data

Wray, T. J.
    Good girls, bad girls : the enduring lessons of twelve women of the
Old Testament / T. J. Wray.
        p. cm.
    Includes bibliographical references and index.
    ISBN-13: 978-0-7425-6251-6 (cloth : alk. paper)
    ISBN-10: 0-7425-6251-4 (cloth : alk. paper)
    ISBN-10: 0-7425-6557-2 (electronic)
    ISBN-13: 978-0-7425-6557-9 (electronic)
    1. Women in the Bible. 2. Bible. O.T.—Biography. I. Title.
BS575.W73 2008
221.9'22082—dc22   2008019230

Printed in the United States of America

♾ ™ The paper used in this publication meets the minimum requirements
of American National Standard for Information Sciences—Permanence of
Paper for Printed Library Materials, ANSI/NISO Z39.48-1992.

With much love to
my amazing daughter,
Annie—
a good girl beyond compare.

Contents

Section Two:
Victims, Volunteers, and Vindicators

Acknowledgments

I WOULD LIKE to thank my wonderful family, especially my children, Bob, Annie, and Jack for their continued love and support. I am also immensely grateful for the many friends who continue to grace my life with joy and encouragement. Special thanks to Walter Burr, the man who started it all; my agent, Rob McQuilkin; and editor, Sarah Stanton, for their enthusiasm and dedication to this important project. Finally, I'd like to express my heartfelt gratitude to the faculty, staff, and especially the wonderful students at Salve Regina University, Catholic Theological Union, and Andover Newton Theological School for their continued affirmation and prayerful support.

Introduction

S EVERAL YEARS AGO, while teaching an undergradu-
ate course on women in the Bible at Salve Regina University, a strange thing happened. As we trudged toward the
end of the spring semester, instead of the anticipated spring
fever absences so common during those first few weeks of
longer days and much-awaited sunshine, my students actually
began arriving *early* for class. Iced lattes in hand, they sat casually in small groups and chatted. As I reviewed my lecture
notes one sunny afternoon, I overheard snippets of an ani-
mated conversation about the infamous Jezebel, the subject of
the day's lecture: "I actually think that Jezebel wasn't as bad
as the biblical writer would have us believe," one student stated
with authority. Another student agreed, "Remember, Jezebel's
a foreigner. Of course she's going to get a bad review from the
author!" To which a third student quipped, "Yeah, she's no
Ruth," followed by a peal of laughter.

I felt so proud I thought I would burst. Just a few months
ago, the same students who now sat discussing the story of
Jezebel like a gaggle of sage rabbis, struggled to make meaning out of the stories of the biblical matriarchs. Here they
were now, coming to class early to discuss the previous night's

readings with their classmates. *Just what is going on here?*, I wondered.

While I would like to claim credit for inspiring the rabbis Lindsay, Sara, Eldon, and Dan with my dazzling lectures, the truth is, they were fascinated by the memorable stories of biblical women whose struggles, triumphs, joys, and sorrows so closely mirror their own. And apparently they are not alone. Courses on women in the Bible have become part of the curriculums of most religious studies/theology departments—at both high school and university levels—and those amazing Bible babes have become a popular choice for ongoing Bible study in temples and churches across the country and abroad.

As we begin our exploration of what biblical scholars refer to as the *women stories* in the Bible, we cannot help but wonder why such a thoroughly patriarchal collection of ancient texts would include so many stories about women in the first place. Of course, the biblical authors did not *invent* patriarchy, for patriarchy was well entrenched in the ancient Near East before a single word of the Bible was ever written. Still, it is a provocative question.

In the past, not much consideration was given to the stories about women in the Bible. The focus was on the male characters and their female counterparts occupied a secondary role, if that. Since many of the women in the Bible are unnamed, it was often assumed that their stories were somehow unimportant—or less important than the stories about men. Within the last several decades, thanks to the pioneering work of (mostly) feminist biblical scholars, archaeologists, historians, and others who have attempted to recover women's stories, the opposite seems to be the case. That is, quite often, it is the *woman's story* that holds the key to unlocking the biblical truth the author sought to impart.

Further, some scholars speculate that the stories about women are actually allegorical, reflecting the status of Israel as a nation. The geographical location of Palestine was both a blessing and a curse. Its location was part of a larger trade route, which facilitated the transmission of stories and ideas from other lands (there are numerous references to other cultures and foreign religious practices in the Bible), but this location also made Israel vulnerable to attacks—not only from the powerful northern empires of Assyria, and later, Babylonia but also from the south (Egypt) and even from beyond her shores (the so-called "Sea Peoples") from the eastern Mediterranean.

Israel, like her women, was often powerless against her enemies, both foreign and domestic. Weak and marginalized nations and people—and the Israelites were no exception—often resort to devious means to survive. Indeed, the ability to draw on one's wit and cunning in a particular situation was highly prized in ancient Israel; in fact, many of Israel's great heroines (and heroes) are revered not for their physical or political prowess, but for their ability to scheme and connive.

It is not surprising, then, that many of the women stories in the Bible feature a trickster type female who is somehow able to manipulate events to bring about a particular outcome. It is important to keep in mind, however, that despite what we might consider less-than-honorable means to an end, the trickster tales are viewed positively because the trickster *brings about God's plan.* Most of the biblical women featured in this book, in one way or another, demonstrate resourcefulness in difficult situations and all of them, in the final analysis, help to bring about God's plan.

I have divided the twelve stories into two rather broad categories. Section One, "Liars, Lawbreakers, and Lovers," contains the stories of the clever Rebekah; Rahab, the hooker with a heart of gold; Samson's lover, Delilah; Ruth, the Moabite; the compassionate medium, the Witch of Endor; and finally, one of the most intriguing (and misunderstood) women in the Hebrew Bible, the infamous Jezebel.

Section Two, "Victims, Volunteers, and Vindicators," begins with story of the widow, Tamar, considered a folk heroine in ancient Israel, followed by the story of Miriam, the sister of Moses, and two stories of sexual abuse, both connected to King

David: Bathsheba, one of David's wives, and his daughter Tamar (not the same Tamar found in Genesis 38, but perhaps named for her). Section Two concludes with the Shunammite woman, an unusual type of female character, who offers hospitality to the prophet Elisha, followed by the inspiring story of Susanna, the falsely accused Jewess who was in the wrong place at the wrong time.

The categories found in each section (Liars, Lawbreakers, and Lovers; Victims, Volunteers, and Vindicators) alert the reader to the kinds of stories found there. This is not to say that all biblical women fall under these six categories, for there are many others (including women as wisdom figures, prophets, and judges) but that the twelve I have selected seem to fit these particular designations. Some of the women have more than one characteristic. For example, Ruth, the Bible's good girl extraordinaire, is *only* a lover while Susanna is *both* a victim and a vindicator.

Why did I choose these particular twelve stories—and why *twelve* stories in the first place? As a professor who has created and fine-tuned her own course on biblical women, I have thought about, researched, and lectured on nearly all of the women in both the Hebrew Bible and the New Testament. I have carefully selected women who are both interesting to read about and who are representative of the *types* of women stories found in the Bible.

The number twelve, of course, is biblically symbolic (e.g., the twelve tribes of Israel and Jesus' twelve apostles); but, while this book examines *twelve stories*, there are actually more than twelve biblical women profiled in *Good Girls, Bad Girls*. This is because, in many cases, the story of one biblical woman is connected to another woman story in the Bible. For example, the story of Delilah cannot be told without also telling the story of the other two unnamed women responsible for Samson's downfall. Likewise, the story of Ruth cannot be told without also telling the story of her mother-in-law, Naomi, to whom Ruth was completely devoted.

This book goes beyond simply telling the story of a particular biblical woman (though the stories alone make the book worth reading) to challenge the reader to explore the enduring lessons the ancient writers sought to impart. These timeless lessons are as important for us today as they were thousands of years ago.

I highly recommend reading the actual story as it appears in the Bible along with this book. While I do not promote one translation of the Bible over another (currently, there are scores of English translations available, from the King James Version to the New English Bible), I have chosen to use the New Oxford Annotated Bible, which uses the New Revised Standard Version, or NRSV. All citations, unless otherwise noted, come from that translation.

There are several issues I will mention at the outset. The first has to do with the use of inclusive language, in particular, the way in which I refer to God (Yhwh). Although there are ample references to God in the Hebrew Bible that are feminine, the overwhelming majority of references reflect the patriarchal assumption at the time that God was male. I have tried to use inclusive language for God when possible and appropriate. There are times, however, when literarily, inclusive language makes reading difficult and confusing—and it deviates from the text and the author's intention. Often, the practice appears contrived and artificial, to the point of making a mockery of the convention. To avoid both confusion and the appearance of political correctness for political correctness's sake, there will be times when I reluctantly resort to the archaic practice of assigning the male pronoun to God.

The second issue has to do with the way in which I refer to the two main sections of the Bible, commonly called the "Old Testament" and the "New Testament." While I will refer to the second main section of the Bible by its common designation, the New Testament, I prefer the term, "Hebrew Bible" rather than Old Testament when referring to the first main section of the Bible. While the terms Old Testament and Hebrew Bible are often used interchangeably, I personally feel the latter designation is not only more accurate, but also more respectful of Judaism. The designation "Old Testament" carries a somewhat negative connotation for many because the adjective "old" implies something outdated and in need of replacement. I decided to use the term Old Testament in the title of this book simply because it is more recognizable among the general public.

In keeping with the conventions of modern historical and biblical scholarship, I will use B.C.E. (Before the Common Era) instead of B.C. (Before Christ) and C.E. (Common Era) rather than A.D. (*Anno Domini*, Latin for "In the year of our Lord") when indicating specific dates.

Finally, in telling each story, I have tried to remain faithful to the thoughts, ideas, and intentions, as well as I may discern them, of the biblical author or authors. This does not mean, however, that my interpretations are definitive. One of the many reasons the Bible has survived for millennia is because various individuals and groups have felt strengthened and nourished by a particular story due to the manner in which they understood it. Indeed, it is my hope that this book, whether read in the classroom, reading groups, as part of a religious education program, or individually, will spark reflection, discussion, and debate. As a teacher, scholar, and person of faith, I cherish the Bible and delight in sharing my passion for Scripture with my many students, and now, with you.

Life for Women during Biblical Times

ANYONE WHO has ever been captivated by the Bible's
women stories can't help but wonder: What was life
really like for women during biblical antiquity? The
more we know about women's day-to-day existence—their
work, how they cared for their families, and how they worshiped their God—the better able we are to more fully appreciate the biblical stories about them. In exploring this basic
question, however, we must first turn our attention to the
world of the ancient Near East, in particular, Israel.

As each story is set within a particular time period, it is
important to have some basic understanding of Israel's complex and fractious history and the key women who help tell
the story of Israel's past. What follows is a brief overview of
the birth of the nation of Israel, according to the Bible. We
must be mindful that the biblical authors, most of whom are
anonymous, sought to convey a *theological* history; that is, a
history based on the people's relationship with God.

Because the biblical writers were primarily interested in
conveying theological truths, as they understood them, they

often seem unconcerned with details, such as why is it that the snake in the Garden of Eden has the power of speech; or just what is the recipe for the manna the Lord provided for the people in the wilderness; or how can postmenopausal Sarah give birth to a son at age ninety? This dearth of detail may prove frustrating for modern readers, eager for such minutiae. It is important to remember, however, that we are wading into the ford of religious literature, where animals sometimes talk, bread rains down from Heaven, and old women have babies.

The Bible relates several pivotal events that seem to have shaped the consciousness and religious perspectives of the people known as Israel. These events begin with the creation of the world and the first humans—Adam and his wife Eve—as narrated in the first three chapters of Genesis. Eve is one of the most misunderstood characters in the Bible. For centuries, she has been portrayed as a temptress, the bad girl who tricked Adam into consuming the forbidden apple, and who ruined the perfectly fine paradise God created for Adam and the animals. A simple reading of Genesis 3, however, reveals that these assertions have no validity whatsoever.

> Now the serpent was more crafty than any other wild animal that the Lord God had made. He said to the woman, "Did God say, 'You shall not eat from any tree in the garden'?" The woman said to the serpent, "We may eat of the fruit of the trees in the garden; but God said, 'You shall not eat of the fruit of the tree that is in the middle of the garden, nor shall you touch it, or you shall die.'" But the serpent said to the woman, "You will not die; for God knows that when you eat of it your eyes will be opened, and you will be like God, knowing good and evil." So when the woman saw that the tree was good for food, and that it was a delight to the eyes, and that the tree was to be desired to make one wise, she

took of its fruit and ate; and she also gave some to her husband, who was with her, and he ate (Gen. 3:1–6).

As we can see, Genesis 3 opens with Eve (*and* Adam) in the Garden having a conversation with the snake. Though she was not yet created when God issues the command to Adam regarding the forbidden fruit (Gen. 2:16–17), she is nonetheless aware that certain trees are off limits. This is an important point, the central point, in fact, that the ancient author sought to convey. For while the text never says that Adam and Eve *sinned*, they nonetheless disobeyed God's command and therefore must be punished.

There are several popular misconceptions about Eve and this story in general, the first of which assumes that the talking snake is the Devil/Satan. The identification of the serpent as Satan is without any foundation in the original story. The snake is simply one of the creatures the Lord created and does not possess any particular qualities of evil. Moreover, the author of this story has no understanding of the concept of an evil being opposed to God. This sort of dualism emerges later—much later—in Jewish and Christian lore. The first association between Satan and the snake comes hundreds of years after the composition of Genesis 3, during the period of time between the testaments, appropriately termed the Intertestamental Period. In certain works written during the Intertestamental Period (200 B.C.E.–200 C.E.), the serpent did come to be identified with Satan, but these are ancient texts that are not part of the Bible.

The only biblical connection we have between the snake and Satan is tenuous, at best, and occurs in the New Testament book of Revelation: ". . . that ancient serpent, who is called the Devil and Satan" (Rev. 12:9); and ". . . the dragon, that ancient serpent, who is called the Devil and Satan" (Rev. 20:2). Of course, it is unclear if the "ancient serpent" refers to the snake in the Garden at all.

The most influential work that connects Satan with the serpent in the Garden of Eden is John Milton's sixteenth century poem, *Paradise Lost*. Milton's popular work of fiction gradually bled into the folklore surrounding Satan and became The Gospel Truth among the biblically illiterate masses. In the same way, the idea that an apple was the forbidden fruit comes from sources outside the Bible. In the early centuries of the Common Era, the Bible began to be translated into Latin. Because the Latin word for "bad" (*malus*) and the word for "apple" (*malum*) sound so similar, the fruit in the Garden came to be identified as an apple, even though Genesis 3 never explicitly states the type of fruit in question.

Another common misconception is that Eve tempted Adam to eat the fruit. Again, a careful reading of the story shows that Adam is with Eve during her conversation with the snake. Adam not only fails to interject a warning regarding the fruit (after all, he alone was the recipient of God's injunction against eating from certain trees (Gen. 2:16–17) but he simply takes the fruit from his wife and eats it: ". . . she took of its fruit and ate; and she also gave some to her husband, who was with her, and he ate" (Gen. 3:6). Clearly, there is no temptation scene of any sort in this story.

The end result of all this confusion is that, for centuries, Eve has been shrilly accused as the one responsible for bringing evil into the world. To be sure, Eve *did* transgress, but Adam is every bit as guilty, a fact often swept aside in sermons and Sunday school discussions that focus on Eve as the sole perpetrator. But if Eve, the first woman mentioned in the Bible, is so misunderstood and her story so misconstrued, how does this bode for other stories featuring women? The distortions of Eve's story are troubling; in light of this, how are we to read the other women stories in the Bible?

At the very least, we must read each story for ourselves, taking text in hand and moving verse by verse. Moreover, we must read each story with a critical eye, flagging questions and inconsistencies. And, at best, we should try to learn something about the time period in which the story was written, the context of the particular story, the woman's relationship to the other characters in the story, and the general scholarly consensus regarding the meaning of the story.

The tale of Adam and Eve is part of the so-called "Primeval History," a collection of stories that span the first eleven chapters of Genesis. Other women featured in the Primeval History are largely nameless, such as the wife of Cain; Noah's wife; and Noah's daughters-in-law. The stories included in the Primeval History express Israel's particular worldview, which holds that God is the author of life, creator of everything, both human and nonhuman, and that the world and all of creation is good.

The call of Abraham, from his home in southern Mesopotamia to the land of Canaan, where he enters into a covenant with God with the divine promises of descendants and the land, is the second major event in the Bible (Gen. 12). The story of Abraham and Sarah is first in a series of tales of Israel's founding fathers and mothers. A childless, elderly couple, they are unlikely leaders; but their obedience in following the Lord's command, a highly prized virtue in the Bible, results in the miracle of a son (Gen. 21:1–3), the author's way of reminding us that with God, all things are possible.

Sarah is an important figure in the unfolding saga of Israel's humble beginnings, even as she is a bit of a contradiction. Though she obediently follows her husband and seems to trust in his strange God, as the years pass, she grows impatient with the Lord's delayed promise of a son and decides to take matters into her own hands. She offers her Egyptian servant, Hagar, to her husband in a sort of proxy pregnancy, but things go terribly wrong (Gen. 16).

Once Hagar becomes pregnant with Abraham's child, she begins to act superior (Gen. 16:4). In her frustration and rage, Sarah abuses Hagar so much that she runs away (Gen. 16:6). Though Hagar eventually returns, she is later banished for good, along with her son, Ishmael, following the birth of

Sarah's own son, Isaac (Gen. 21:9–9). Of course, all of this does not paint a very flattering portrait of the first biblical matriarch. But Sarah's mercurial personality, her vacillating trust in God, and her all-too-human failings remind us that God loves us despite our imperfections, a theme that reverberates throughout the Hebrew Bible.

Isaac, the son of the promise, marries Rebekah, a woman known for her cleverness and trickery (see chapter 1), and together they have twin sons, Jacob and Esau (Gen. 25:23–26). God designates Jacob as the one who will continue the original promise made to Abraham (Gen. 25:23), and Rebekah sees to it that Jacob, *not* her other son, Esau, fulfills his destiny. Rebekah's preferential treatment of Jacob and, consequently, Isaac's favored treatment of Esau, sets into motion a sibling rivalry subplot, also a favorite theme of the biblical authors.

Jacob grows up and becomes a trickster character, just like his mother. He marries sisters Leah, a homely but exceedingly fertile girl, and Rachel, Leah's beautiful, shapely sibling, who captures Jacob's heart. Again, we have the sibling rivalry motif as the two compete for Jacob's attention even as they compete to produce children. Rachel, like Sarah and Rebekah before her, experiences temporary barrenness. Though she is eventually blessed with a son—Joseph, who will be the last in the line of biblical patriarchs—Rachel dies giving birth to her second son, Benjamin. Leah, unlike her sister, has many children, six sons and a daughter, Dinah.

The sons of Jacob become the founders of the twelve tribes of Israel. A mere two generations after Abraham, his grandson Jacob, later known as "Israel," will leave his famine-stricken home in Canaan for Egypt, along with his sons, thus setting the stage for Israel's epic tale of liberation that begins in the book of Exodus. According to Exodus, the Israelites migrate to Egypt in search of food. There, they not only find food, but they also find that Egyptian life agrees with them, at least for a time. They settle in and then, for reasons that are unclear, become the slaves of an unnamed Egyptian Pharaoh (Exod. 1:1–14).

The book of Exodus opens with the midwives, Shiphrah and Puah, who disobey Pharaoh's command to kill all Hebrew baby boys upon delivery. Pharaoh issued this command fearing the boys will grow up and make war. The midwives' disobedience paves the way for the Bible's greatest liberator, Moses. Other women involved in preserving young Moses' life include his mother, Jochebed, who hides the infant Moses from the Egyptian authorities, and his sister, Miriam (chapter 8), who protects him after his mother places him in a basket and sets him afloat on the Nile (Exod. 2:1–4). Pharaoh's daughter is also involved in his rescue, for it is she who draws him from the river and raises him as her adopted son (Exod. 2:5–10).

Thanks to these women, Moses not only survives but he will be called by God to free the Israelites from slavery, leading them on a forty-year trek to Canaan. Along the way, at the pilgrimage site of Mount Sinai, Moses receives the Torah (the "Teaching"), the religious legal code that binds the people of Israel to their God (Exod. 20). Though Moses is a towering biblical figure, he will not enter the Promised Land (Exod. 32:48–52; 34:7). Rather, it is under the leadership of Joshua, Moses' successor, that the children of Israel finally take possession of the land flowing with milk and honey. The Canaanite prostitute, Rahab (chapter 2), stands at the threshold of Israel's conquest of the land and becomes the first convert in the Promised Land (Josh. 2:11).

So now we have the creation of the world, a community ethic (commonly known as the Ten Commandments), and the Israelites living in the Promised Land. This seems like the end of the story—but the tale is only just beginning. At first, Israel lives in the land under a loose tribal federation led by judges. The book of Judges is a blood-and-guts collection of stories that features several prominent women, including Deborah, a prophetess and judge, and Jael, the woman who murders one of Israel's oppressors by driving a tent peg through his skull (Judg. 4–5).

Another famous judge, Samson, is an oversexed, impulsive young man who displays a weakness for Philistine females. Samson is best described as the Bible's version of a superhero, who can kill a lion with his bare hands (Judg. 14:6) and slaughter a thousand men with the jawbone of an ass (Judg. 15:15–16). The source of his super strength is his uncut hair, a secret he shares with no one—until he falls in love with Delilah (chapter 3). In a moment of weakness, Delilah is able to coax from Samson his secret and then she promptly betrays him to his enemies (Judg. 16:15–22).

The brutality of the book of Judges is mediated somewhat by the book that follows it in the canon, the book of Ruth (chapter 4). The book of Ruth is basically a love story and it is perhaps the only book in the Bible in which all the characters behave themselves. The two key women in the story are Naomi, Ruth's mother-in-law, and her Moabite daughter-in-law, Ruth. Theirs is a most unusual mother-in-law/daughter-in-law relationship, then and now, for the pair travel together, protect each other, and demonstrate genuine love and affection for one another. The book of Ruth is placed in the canon before the books of Samuel because of Ruth's connection to the great King David—her son, Obed, is David's grandfather.

The next major event in the history of Israel is the institution of the monarchy. Wanting to be like the other nations, Israel demands from God a king, the first of whom is Saul (1 Sam. 8–9). And, though the new king begins well, due to a series of inept decisions and cultic violations, he experiences a slow spiral downward (1 Sam. 11; 15). The text attributes this fall from grace to the Lord, who sends a "tormenting spirit" to torture poor Saul (1 Sam. 16:14). He becomes extremely paranoid, highly agitated, and completely irrational. With the Philistines on the move, Saul must pull himself together to fight. He frantically consults the Lord, but receives only silence. In desperation, he turns to a medium, the Witch of Endor (chapter 5) for help in conjuring the ghost of the dead prophet, Samuel, for advice (1 Sam. 28:8–25).

Though Saul himself forbade the use of sorcery, he has nowhere else to turn (1 Sam. 28:3). The witch is successful in calling forth Samuel but there will be no happy ending. Samuel's stark prediction that Saul and his sons will die in battle the next day comes to sad fruition.

David assumes the throne after Saul's death and, despite his many flaws, is God's unrivaled favorite against whom all other future kings are measured. While David is a visionary ruler who unites the nation, his personal life is in shambles. David makes several serious mistakes in judgment that eventually destroy both his family and ultimately, his kingship. His downfall begins when he decides to bed Bathsheba (chapter 8), who is married to one of David's loyal soldiers, Uriah the Hittite (2 Sam. 11–12). Other men's wives are of no concern to the king, for he takes what he wants.

When Bathsheba becomes pregnant with David's child, the king attempts to cover his crime and arranges to have Uriah killed in battle (1 Sam. 11–12). Once Uriah is out of the way, David marries Bathsheba and together they have a son. Foolishly, David believes he has gotten away with his crimes but the Lord disagrees (2 Sam. 11:27). Though David repents, the Lord's punishment is severe: four of David's sons will die because of the sins of their father (2 Sam. 12:18).

With his family near ruin, David dies, a pathetic old king, and is succeeded by his son, Solomon (1 Kings 1:38–40), who builds the great Temple in Jerusalem and is remembered as a wise king with a penchant for foreign women.

The rise and fall of the monarchy (1–2 Sam. and 1–2 Kings) continues with a parade of mostly despicable kings, including King Ahab and his Phoenician wife, Jezebel (chapter 6), who practice every form of social injustice imaginable. Accordingly, God sends his prophets to call the kings to task. Acting as the Lord's mouthpiece on Earth, the prophet warns the king and the people to repent and return to the Lord, or else. The theme of *remembering* is a common prophetic concern. The king and the people should *remember* the God who saves them; *remember* their covenant with this God and to live up to the terms of the covenant; and *remember* to act justly.

There are the so-called "writing prophets," those who have purportedly written books themselves or through scribes, and the "nonwriting prophets," who appear in various biblical passages, usually as part of a longer narrative written by someone other than the prophet. Samuel (1–2 Sam.), Nathan (2 Sam. and 1 Kings), Elijah, and Elisha (1–2 Kings) are examples of nonwriting prophets who nonetheless share most of the same concerns as the writing prophets.

The writing prophets appear in sixteen books named after sixteen prophets. Depending on the size of their books or scrolls at the time of the biblical writing, they are considered either a "major" or "minor" prophet. This designation, of course, does not mean that one prophet is more important than another, only that some prophetic works are longer than another. There are four Major Prophets (Isaiah, Jeremiah, Ezekiel, and Daniel) and twelve Minor Prophets (Hosea, Joel, Amos, Obadiah, Jonah, Micah, Nahum, Habakkuk, Zephaniah, Haggai, Zechariah, and Malachi).

In addition to the named prophets, there are scores of anonymous prophets, like the stable of prophets, usually called "guild prophets," who assemble to interpret dreams and offer advice to the king. In fact, we can note a flurry of prophetic activity around the monarchy, but as the monarchy disappears by the fifth century B.C.E., prophecy also disappears. Though the reasons for this decline remain unclear, we do know that the prophets appear on the scene to address political or ethical crises resulting from a largely despotic monarchal system. While most prophets are male, there are exceptions, most notably Moses' older sister, Miriam (Exod. 15:20, Num. 12), the popular judge, Deborah (Judg. 4–5) and Huldah (2 Kings 22:14–20), who is called upon to authenticate an ancient scroll ("the book of the law") found in the Temple during restoration efforts initiated by King Josiah (640–609 B.C.E.).

The failure to heed prophetic warnings results in the loss of the land—first to the Assyrians, who attack the northern kingdom of Samaria in 721 B.C.E., and then to the Babylonians, who invade Judah to the south and capture Jerusalem in 587 B.C.E. Both of these events are narrated in some detail in the Bible, but it is the Babylonian invasion under King Nebuchadnezzar and the subsequent exile of the Jewish people of Israel to Babylon that is considered perhaps the most the pivotal event in the Hebrew Bible. In fact, when we speak of the two general time periods in the Hebrew Bible, we generally refer to them as either "pre-exilic" or "post-exilic." Although the exiles, under an edict of liberation from the Persian king, Cyrus, eventually return to the Promised Land, their problems are far from over.

The roughly 200 years of rather benign Persian rule was followed by the Greek period (332–63 B.C.E.). Hellenistic culture was introduced and flourished in many parts of the Near East, including much of Palestine. Following the death of Alexander the Great in 32 B.C.E., Judea was ruled by the despised Antiochus IV, a Syrian whose violent persecutions of pious Jews is described in grisly detail in the books of 1–2 Maccabees, found in the Apocrypha. This persecution resulted in a revolt and a brief period of Judean self rule (142–63 B.C.E.).

In 63 B.C.E., Pompey and his Roman soldiers conquered Judea, absorbing her as part of the Roman Empire for the next 130 years. Jesus of Nazareth would live and die under Roman rule and eventually the Jews would rebel against the Romans. Sadly, this rebellion resulted in the total destruction of the Promised Land in 70 C.E.

Israel's tumultuous history serves as the backdrop for the women stories in the Bible. As we read the stories of biblical women, we must remember that women's lives were greatly affected by invasions, foreign rule, and the general unrest that characterized ancient Israel. Concerns about their children, their homes, and the realities of war and unrest surely occupied their thoughts and influenced their decisions. Armed with this general overview of Israel's history, let us now narrow our focus to explore the daily lives of women during biblical antiquity.

The Bible offers scant details about how women lived, worked, and existed within the patriarchal culture that governed much of their behavior. Fortunately, however, during the past several decades, extrabiblical sources, both written and archeological, have helped us begin to understand more about the lives of women during the first millenium. Archeological excavations, in particular, have given us new insights into the world of the ancient Near East, and have enabled us to see where women lived, the homes and neighborhoods where they worked and took care of their families. Artifacts, such as pots, tools, and jewelry have been unearthed that allow us to imagine the hands that fashioned them, used them, and treasured them.

Although the portrait of women's lives during biblical antiquity remains an incomplete canvas, there are some aspects of their daily lives that we can sketch with reasonable certainty. In general, we know that life for most women was challenging, arduous, and brief. Much of the peasant population worked long hours in less than desirable conditions; many were malnourished, and most died young.

The overwhelming majority of women (estimates vary, but probably around ninety percent) lived in rural villages, in agricultural settings. They lived in simple dwellings; some lived in tents or even caves, but many lived in crude houses, either one or two stories, made of mud brick or stone with a roof. There were no glass windows, but most houses were equipped with shutters. The home would be simply adorned and functional. The roof was a very important feature, for not only did it keep the home cool and dry, but it was also used for sleeping, bathing, and drying fruit or flax. Two of the stories in this book feature important "roof scenes." Rahab hides the Israelite spies on her roof under drying flax (Josh. 2:6) and

Bathsheba becomes the object of David's lust when he sees her bathing on her roof (2 Sam. 11:2).

Though most women lived in rural areas, a small percentage of women lived in more urban settings, mainly in or around the capital, Jerusalem. Many city houses were built into the wall that surrounded the city and some were more luxurious than others.

There was a marked contrast—as there is in contemporary society—between the country wife and the city wife. Urban dwellers in ancient Israel were often more affluent; the work was less backbreaking and, consequently, they typically lived longer. Women who lived in cities were often the wives of priests, businessmen, merchants, or political figures. The availability of goods and services in the city would naturally make life simpler for women, though her role as wife and mother would be strikingly similar to those women who lived in villages. Since the majority of women lived in rural areas, our focus will be on their lifestyle, though much of what can be said about them—especially with regard to marriage and motherhood—can likewise be said about women who lived in cities.

Marriage was considered the natural state for men and women and although there are certainly instances where Israelite men (and, to a lesser extent, Israelite women) were not married, this was the exception rather than the norm. Most women married quite young, usually soon after the onset of menstruation, which of course, heralded fertility. Marriages were usually brokered between families and most women had little or no say in the matter. The idea of romantic love, as we understand it today, was not typically a consideration in arranged marriages. Men usually married later (in their twenties or even thirties) and thus most men were older than their wives. Since the life expectancy for women was shorter than for men (for rural women, thirty; rural men, forty) this arrangement made sense.

Girls were expected to remain virgins until they were married. Virginity was highly prized in ancient Israel, not only because of its religious implications, but also because virginity indicated a certain measure of self-control and obedience, qualities desirable in a wife and predictive of marital fidelity.

This is not to imply that *all* women were virgins when they married; indeed, it is likely that some were not. If a husband suspected that his wife was not a virgin on their wedding night, he could reject her, which would be a great humiliation for both the new bride and her family. Of course, her family was not without recourse.

If parents could offer evidence that their daughter was indeed a virgin, in the form of a bloody marital sheet (Deut. 22:13–21), then her husband would not be allowed to divorce her. Setting aside the way in which the parents obtained said sheet, if the elders of the town (an all-male legal tribunal whose task it was to render legal decisions and settle disputes) examined the sheet and found evidence of the woman's virginity, then the husband would be fined and his request for divorce denied. Divorce consisted of little more than a written notice to the woman that she had been divorced. If, however, the town elders found in favor of the aggrieved husband, then the woman would be brought to her father's house and stoned to death by the townsmen.

Assuming she passed the virginity test, the new bride and her husband would likely view sex as an important aspect of marriage. In fact, a newly married man could be granted a leave of absence for up to a year from military service or business to concentrate on his lovemaking skills (Deut. 24:5), a biblical precedent that could no doubt contribute to contemporary marital harmony!

Shortly after marriage, a woman would assume all of the duties expected of a wife, including maintaining the home and bearing and raising children. Her days would be long, literally from sunup to sundown, and filled with many chores and responsibilities. She would rise early, typically before the rest of the family, and light the fires for the day. Next, she would procure water, gathering her water jars and walking, sometimes miles, to the town well. Once at the town well, she would have to wait her turn, along with the other women, to draw water. Most town wells were not the cute bricked-and-bucketed wells of storybooks; they were usually located at the bottom of a long, often circuitous shaft, which required the woman to climb down a dark, narrow passageway, fill her heavy ceramic jars, and then lug those jars back home. Though many homes also had backyard cisterns that gathered rainwater, these were insufficient to meet most families' demands and were dry most of the year in the hot, arid climate so characteristic of much of Israel.

Women were also in charge of grinding wheat into flour, kneading and baking bread, a time-consuming task, to be sure. She was also responsible for cooking and serving meals, cleaning the house, making and mending clothing, tending to the family livestock (which usually consisted of a few sheep and perhaps a cow that lodged in the front part of the house), and assisting her husband during the harvest. A woman's primary role and duty, however, was that of mother.

Women were expected to have many children, and children were viewed as cherished gifts from God. It was considered unnatural not to want or have children. Despite the high infant mortality rate (scholars speculate that as many as half of all children never reached adulthood) and great personal risk (maternal deaths were a leading cause of death for women, mainly from complications during childbirth and postpartum infections), it is clear that most women very much wanted to become mothers.

The Bible seems to indicate a preference for sons; this may be due, in part, to the practicalities of agrarian life and the ancestral inheritance of land passed from father to son, (Num. 27:8–11). Aside from societal expectations and the innate desire to have children, motherhood was a way for women to gain social acceptance and some measure of status and power. This was especially true for mothers of powerful sons.

With children, of course, came added responsibilities and duties. Children remained at home with their mothers until about age five, when boys were considered old enough to begin to work alongside their fathers in the fields. Daughters generally remained at home to learn the skills necessary to someday become capable wives and mothers. Before that time, children were required to help with household chores and learn the social skills necessary to live and work within the community.

Since most children were raised in local villages without access to public education, it seems likely that women were responsible for the early education of children, including their religious education (Deut. 11:19–21; 31:46). This means that it was the mother who handed down the cherished religious traditions from generation to generation, even as they were denied positions of power within the Temple hierarchy.

While children were considered great blessings from God, what can be said of those who were not so blessed? Barrenness was seen as a terrible curse and was always the "fault" of the woman. In the ancient world, the medical causes of infertility were unknown and male sterility was rarely, if ever, considered to be the cause of the problem. Hence, the barren woman not only felt incomplete in her expected roles as wife and mother, but she was also socially ostracized and the likely victim of sideway glances, gossip, and ridicule among the townspeople.

Worse still, barrenness was viewed as form of divine punishment which, of course, only added to a woman's stigmatization. Every barren couple must have searched for reasons why God would withhold children from them and one can only imagine the pain and suffering they must have endured, thinking that they had somehow offended God to such an extent that God felt compelled to punish them so severely. Barrenness is a common theme in the Bible; for example, each of the matriarchs Sarah, Rebekah, Rachel, and Leah was barren at some point—that is, until God, who alone opens and closes all wombs, miraculously removed their barrenness. These stories all have a predictable pattern and usually end with the blessing of a long-awaited son, a sign of God's favor. Such stories may have offered hope to childless couples, but probably did little to mitigate the day-to-day longing, guilt, and sorrow that surely accompanied infertility.

In an androcentric society, where men created and enforced the laws, dominated religious and political life, and had the final say in matters pertaining to all facets of family life, one might logically wonder if a woman had any ability to determine her own destiny. Although the Bible seems to insinuate that all women were subordinate to men, there are many women stories that indicate the opposite. It is clear that many women thought for themselves and acted on their own accord (or some might argue, under divine directive), without the advice, permission, or the blessings of a man. Hence, the women stories present us with a bit of a paradox. On the one hand, the Bible is undeniably steeped in patriarchy—a cultural reality that is necessarily restrictive, subjugating, and even misogynistic. On the other hand, there are stories in the Bible that feature women taking matters into their own capable hands and making decisions independent of men.

What are we to do with such a paradox? At one end of a rather wide spectrum is a traditional, undeniably conservative interpretation of the women stories that would advocate contemporary adherence to the patriarchal norms found in the Bible. Many religiously conservative groups, both Jewish and Christian, embrace these norms and women are required to strictly follow many of the patriarchal dictates found in the Bible. At the other end of this spectrum is the tendency by some to dismiss the Bible as archaic, outdated, and of little value to women's (and men's) contemporary roles within the family and community.

Perhaps the best way to address this paradox is with a more centralist view. That is, to read the women stories in the Bible for enjoyment, inspiration, and for the pearls of wisdom the biblical author or authors sought to impart. It is clear that the editors of the Hebrew Bible included the women stories so that we might learn something from them. In fact, I often challenge my own students to read a particular biblical story with three central questions in mind:

What is the author trying to teach me about God?
What is the author trying to teach me about myself?
What is the author trying to teach me about others?

It is these questions that are surely important to all of us, regardless of where we might locate ourselves on the spectrum.

As you read the women stories, try to put aside any preconceived notions you may have about a particular woman and simply allow the text to tell the story. Our brains are often repositories of misinformation, collected from confused Sunday school teachers, misunderstood sermons, and parents who mean well, but somehow get the facts wrong. A case in point is Eve, mentioned earlier. And so I challenge you to approach each story with fresh eyes. Of course, some of the women stories may confuse, offend, or disturb modern readers when viewed within the context of contemporary notions of justice and equality. We must, however, remain mindful of the historical, social, political, and religious realities that frame each story and in most cases, we must attempt to look beyond these constraints to mine the rich wisdom the biblical author sought to impart. While the lessons gleaned from these pages may be different for each of us, the enchanting tales of our foremothers in faith are sure to fascinate, delight, and inspire.

Liars, Lawbreakers, and Lovers

Rebekah, Rahab, Delilah, Ruth, The Witch of Endor, and Jezebel

"Many women have done excellently,
but you surpass them all"
(Prov. 31:29).

Rebekah: Lover and Liar
A Woman with a Plan

(Gen. 24:10–67; 26:6–16; 27:5–38; 28:5–6; 29:12–13;
35:8; 49:31)

Now Rebekah was listening when Isaac spoke to his son Esau.
So when Esau went to the field to hunt for game and bring
it, Rebekah said to her son Jacob, "I heard your father say to your
brother Esau, 'Bring me game, and prepare for me savory food to
eat, that I may bless you before the Lord before I die.' Now therefore, my son, obey my word as I command you. Go to the flock,
and get me two choice kids, so that I may prepare from them
savory food for your father, such as he likes; and you shall take it
to your father to eat, so that he may bless you before he dies." But
Jacob said to his mother Rebekah, "Look, my brother Esau is a
hairy man, and I am a man of smooth skin. Perhaps my father will
feel me, and I shall seem to be mocking him, and bring a curse on
myself and not a blessing." His mother said to him, "Let your
curse be on me, my son; only obey my word, and go, get them for
me." So he went and got them and brought them to his mother;
and his mother prepared savory food, such as his father loved.
Then Rebekah took the best garments of her elder son Esau,

which were with her in the house, and put them on her younger
son Jacob; and she put the skins of the kids on his hands and on
the smooth part of his neck. Then she handed the savory food,
and the bread that she had prepared, to her son Jacob (Gen.
27:5–17).

BIBLE READERS throughout the ages have delighted in the story of Rebekah, whose cleverness and single-minded devotion to her son, Jacob, ensures the continuation of God's promise to Abraham. This promise (Gen. 12:2–3) assures the acquisition of the land, an enduring relationship with God who will extol blessings upon future generations, and a proliferation of descendents. The second of the matriarchal figures, preceded by Sarah and followed by Rachel and Leah, Rebekah is one of the most highly developed characters in the Hebrew Bible. She is beautiful, resourceful, and strong-willed; but above all, she is a trickster—a type of character in the Bible, both admired and respected in the ancient world for their skillful use of manipulation to bring about God's plan.

Before we begin to explore Rebekah's story, a general comment regarding the stories of the patriarchs and matriarchs seems in order. In the past, there was a tendency to read the stories of the patriarchs and matriarchs (Abraham and Sarah; Isaac and Rebekah; Jacob and Rachel and Leah) from a strictly "founding fathers," perspective. In recent years, however, scholars have recognized the important role the "founding mothers" played in Israel's beginnings. It is clear that the biblical writers felt that the founding mothers were every bit as important (and some might argue even more important since it is often *their* actions that bring about God's plan) in the formation of the people of Israel. How do we know this? First, the very fact that the matriarchs are included at all is noteworthy. Although the Bible did not invent patriarchy, it is nonetheless the social umbrella under which the women stories are written. To include women—alongside men—in the foundational story of the nascent nation is therefore highly significant.

Second, all of the matriarchs, and many of the women associated with them, such as their maids, are named in the text. Since the overwhelming majority of women in the Hebrew Bible are *not* named, referred to instead as the wife, daughter, mother, or concubine of a named male (e.g., Noah's wife; Lot's daughters; Samson's mother; Gideon's concubine), or in association with a particular place, task, or function (e.g., the prostitute of Gaza; the maidens going out to draw water; the nurse of Joash) naming is a critical detail not to be overlooked.

Finally, the matriarchs are presented not as merely the wives of great men, but as movers and shakers in their own right, outwitting, outsmarting, and outmaneuvering many of the male characters in the stories. This is surely the case with Rebekah, who occupies a more commanding presence in the Bible than her husband, Isaac. It is Rebekah, not Isaac, who will go to great lengths to preserve the continuation of God's promise to Abraham. With these important facts in mind, let us now turn to Rebekah's story.

Rebekah is the only woman in the Hebrew Bible whose birth is actually recorded—coming just after the terrifying tale of the binding of Isaac, and just before the mention of Sarah's death (Gen. 22:23). Placing her birth announcement between these two pivotal events not only situates her in the life of Isaac, but it is the biblical writer's way of honoring her and elevating her to a position of great prominence.

Moreover, the connection between Abraham, considered the founder of the people of Israel, and his grandniece, Rebekah, also accents her important role in the unfolding story of Israel. For example, Rebekah, like Abraham, demonstrates great courage and faith, as she travels from her home in Mesopotamia to Canaan to face an uncertain future (Gen. 12:1; 22:7 and 24:4, 38, 60). Both Abraham and Rebekah enjoy a personal, efficacious relationship with the Lord—who speaks directly to them and to whom they are dedicated. And, the same promise reiterated to Abraham is likewise promised to Rebekah (Gen. 22:17; 24:60).

Rebekah also has much in common with her predecessor, Sarah. Like Sarah, she leaves her homeland and faces many years of barrenness before God bestows the blessings of children. Both Sarah and Rebekah are designated as their husband's sisters in order to save their respective husband's necks, when, in these remarkably similar tales, the promise is severely compromised by the patriarchs. In the first such story (Gen. 12:10–20), Abraham and Sarah journey to Egypt in search of food during a famine. Afraid that Pharaoh will kill him in order to take his wife, Abraham asks Sarah to pretend she is his sister. Pharaoh thinks Sarah is beautiful and brings her into his harem, giving Abraham a tidy sum for giving up his "sister." God, however, is unhappy with this arrangement and, in a foreshadowing of the Exodus story, sends plagues upon Pharaoh. Understandably, Pharaoh is furious with Abraham, not to mention the plagues sent by Abraham's God, and kicks the two out of Egypt.

This type of story reappears in Genesis 20, but this time it is the Philistine King of Gerar, Abimelech, who pays off Abraham and brings the lovely Sarah into his home. Never mind the fact that Sarah is now well into her sixties, a minor biblical detail. In a dream, God tips off the king and Abraham's trickery is revealed.

In a strikingly similar story, Isaac and Rebekah migrate to Gerar to live among the Philistines during yet another famine, a common theme is the Bible, and because of Rebekah's beauty, Isaac, like Abraham, fears the townsmen may kill him in order to get his wife. Isaac passes off Rebekah as his sister, and all is well until the king of the Philistines looks out his window and witnesses Isaac fondling his "sister" and realizes the ruse (Gen. 26:1–12).

These and other similarities between Sarah, Abraham, and Rebekah serve to connect the contiguous tales of the matriarchs and patriarchs, but they also draw our attention to the matriarchs, and their important role in the history of Israel.

Biblical scholars often refer to Rebekah's story as a novella, for it is very much a contained unit, or mini-novel. Her story begins in Genesis 24, the longest chapter in the book of Genesis, with a wooing scene. A common "type scene" (stories that are similar in structure and content) in the Bible, most wooing scenes take place at or near a well, considered a symbol of fertility in the Bible. The "wooer," a servant sent by Abraham to procure a wife for Isaac among Abraham's kinsmen in Haran, stops after his long journey from Canaan, to rest and water his camels. Sending Isaac himself is out of the question; Abraham makes sure that Isaac, the future patriarch and continuation of the promise, remains firmly in Canaan. It is at the well that Abraham's servant meets the subject of his quest, Rebekah, who is, quite literally, the answer to the servant's prayers (Gen. 14:12–21).

She is young, fair, a *betulah* (a virgin of marriageable age), from Abraham's tribe, and, perhaps most important, she fulfills the sign for which the servant prayed:

> "Let the girl to whom I shall say, 'Please offer your jar
> that I may drink' and who shall say, 'Drink, and I will
> water your camels'—let her be the one who you have
> appointed for your servant, Isaac" (Gen. 24:14).

Rebekah not only offers the weary servant a drink from her water jar, but she also fetches water for ten tired and thirsty camels, a task that requires many trips to and from the well. As if this were not enough, Rebekah offers the servant and his animals lodging for the night. Rebekah thus demonstrates both hospitality and a generous spirit, two traits held in the highest regard in the ancient world.

The servant must be overjoyed to learn that Rebekah is from Abraham's lineage (she is the daughter of Abraham's nephew, Bethuel), for this is a prerequisite set forth by Abraham. The other condition for marriage is the woman's willingness to relocate to Canaan, the sacred place the Lord set aside for the people of Israel, and Rebekah will fulfill this requirement as well. The servant must meet Rebekah's family so that the details of the engagement can be worked out. Rebekah dashes off ahead of him, sporting a new nose ring and gold bracelets, gifts from her proxy suitor, to tell her "mother's household" of the exciting encounter at the well. In no time at all, negotiations take place between Rebekah's brother, Laban, the apparent man of the house, and Abraham's servant. That Laban is in the position to arrange his sister's marriage, coupled with the fact that the author refers to Rebekah's home as her "mother's household," seems to indicate that Rebekah's father is absent or even deceased (Gen. 24:28–29).

The servant opens negotiations by first relating his serendipitous encounter with Rebekah at the well—carefully choosing his words so as to indicate the Lord's involvement in the meeting. Both men agree that this is a match made in heaven and, in a curious departure from the patriarchal norms that govern arranged marriages, Rebekah's brother and mother actually *ask* her if she wishes to leave with the servant (Gen. 24:57–58). Rebekah is a woman who knows what she wants— and it seems clear that in her mother's household, she was raised to speak her mind—so Rebekah consents and is on her way to a new life.

Upon her arrival in the Negev, it is Rebekah who first spies Isaac from a distance. She jumps off her camel to get a closer look as he walks toward them in the field, and apparently likes what she sees. Rebekah is brought into "Sarah's tent" (a euphemism for marriage) and consoles Isaac in his bereavement. Noteworthy is Rebekah's move from her "mother's household" to "Sarah's tent" (Gen. 24:28, 67), two facts that act as bookends in Rebekah's migration story. As she leaves one strong woman and begins to try to fill the shoes of another, we have little doubt that she is up to the challenge.

There is one other striking detail in Genesis 24. The author tells us that *Isaac loved Rebekah*: "He took Rebekah, and she became his wife; and he loved her" (Gen. 24:67). In brokered marriages, love was rarely a consideration. This touching detail is a rare one in the Bible, but one that makes the story of Rebekah and Isaac something of a love story.

But, alas, there is nothing like a couple of kids to mess up a perfectly good love story. After twenty years of barrenness, Rebekah conceives twin sons, whose in utero jostling portends their future conflict. Rebekah—without the usual male intercession on her behalf—asks the Lord about the brawling in her belly, and the Lord responds with an oracle:

"Two nations are in your womb,
and two peoples born of you
shall be divided;
the one shall be stronger than the
other;
the elder shall serve the
younger" (Gen. 25:23).

For Rebekah, fulfillment of this divine oracle will become the driving force behind her future actions. Her life's mission henceforth is to ensure the continuation of the promise through her "younger" son, Jacob. The Bible does not tell us if she shared this oracle with Isaac, but it seems likely that she did. After all, he is her husband and they are in love. Moreover, Isaac, more than anyone, understands what it means to be the bearer of the promise.

Rebekah's sons are born in a manner befitting their future roles and a story of sibling rivalry, a popular theme in the Bible, begins. Twin son number two, Jacob (his name in Hebrew, appropriately, means *supplanter*), emerges gripping the heel of his brother, Esau, who is described as a hairy, red baby and the future progenitor of the Edomites. The Edomites are the on-again, off-again enemies of the Israelites. The play on the Hebrew words—red (*'admoi*) and hairy (*se'ar*) are calculated insults aimed at the Edomites, whom the Israelites characterized as a band of hairy thugs who dwelt in the land of red sand. Biblical Edom is located in modern Jordan and, for the record, the sand really is red. The supposed hirsute appearance of the

Edomites, however, cannot be verified; if true, let us hope this quality was confined to the male Edomites.

The twins have very little in common, starting with the striking differences in their physical appearances: Jacob is "smooth-faced" while Esau is furry. Esau is presented as a dull, wild man who likes to hunt; Jacob, on the other hand, is a mama's boy who likes to "keep to his tents" and involve himself in more domestic chores, like cooking. His culinary skills prove profitable when he casually offers his brother some lentil soup in exchange for Esau's birthright. Esau's status as first-born entitles him to certain rights and privileges upon his father's death, including a sizable inheritance and head-of-household status. This also means that Esau would be the one who continues the promise God made to Abraham, something that Rebekah will not allow to happen. Famished from a day in the fields, Esau, a man more interested in his stomach than the lofty responsibilities of a first-born son, readily gives away his birthright for the soup (Gen. 25:29–34).

Apparently, Esau can still gain his inheritance if he receives his father's final blessing. It is in this scene that Rebekah reveals her talents as trickster. Isaac, old and blind and on his death bed, asks his favorite son, Esau, to hunt and prepare a meal for his father so that Isaac can bestow his blessings upon Esau. Rebekah, like many women in the biblical world, gathers information by eavesdropping. When she learns of Isaac's plan to give Esau the blessing, she quickly hatches a plan of her own and, after enlisting the help of Jacob, together they pull off one of the Bible's most amazing hoodwinkings.

Mother and son take kids from the goatherd, prepare a meal for Isaac, and disguise Jacob in his brother's gamey smelling clothes. But Jacob worries that if his father should reach out to touch him, the deception would be known. Not to worry! Clever Rebekah places the hide of the kids on her son's neck and arms to give him the wooly feel of Esau. Clad in his makeshift Esau costume, Jacob approaches Isaac.

Although initially suspicious, Isaac seems to accept the pseudo-Esau, despite the fact that the "voice is Jacob's" and he bestows the blessing upon Jacob. Later, Esau lumbers in from the field and presents his father with *his* meal, only to find that Jacob has once again supplanted him and taken his blessing. Esau is initially heartbroken, but then, furious and vows to kill his brother.

Once again, Rebekah steps in to preserve the promise: Jacob must be sent away and kept at a safe distance from Esau. Rebekah decides that Jacob should flee to her brother Laban's home in Haran (Gen. 27:42–45). Of course, given the restrictions of a patriarchal system—a system that would require fathers (not mothers) to send off children to distant lands with paternal blessings—Rebekah must first convince Isaac that this is a good idea. So, she dramatically complains to Isaac about the unsuitability of the local girls (the Hittite women) for her precious Jacob.

> Then Rebekah said to Isaac, "I am weary of my life because of the Hittite women. If Jacob marries one of the Hittite women such as these, one of the women of the land, what good would my life be to me?" (Gen. 27:46).

Isaac loves Rebekah; if her concerns over the Hittite women are so great that her life would not be worth living should Jacob marry one, Isaac has no choice other than to send Jacob away to marry a decent girl from his own clan. Thus, Isaac gives Jacob the requisite blessings, and off Jacob goes to Mesopotamia (Gen. 28:1–5). The story ends on a somewhat amusing note: Esau, in an effort to spite his father, marries a Canaanite woman (Gen. 28:6–9). Canaanite women are taboo and good Israelite boys should select wives from within their own tribes. To marry a foreign woman is a source of shame for the entire family, most especially one's parents.

While the story exemplifies the lengths to which Rebekah will go to make sure that Jacob prevails, there are two ways scholars have traditionally thought of this story. The first is that Isaac—old, blind, and feeble—is easily fooled into believing that Jacob is really Esau. After all, his wife and son are expert tricksters.

The second way to read this story is with the supposition that Isaac knows all along that Jacob and Rebekah are in collusion. He merely plays along, knowing full well that, although he prefers Esau (never mind the bad parenting going on here with Isaac and Rebekah playing favorites), it is *Jacob* who represents the future of Israel. He therefore allows Rebekah and Jacob to go through their ridiculous ruse.

Any parent, even the old and the blind, knows his or her child's voice and touch. While it's true that the Isaac of Scripture is a bit of an enigma—largely because his character is eclipsed by the antics of his wife and son—he's no idiot. It seems reasonable to assume that he is also aware of his wife's penchant for trickery. It would therefore come as no surprise to him to find Rebekah lurking around the corner eavesdropping on conversations.

If this is the case, we might even go so far as to suggest that Isaac pulled a little stunt of his own and staged the whole conversation with Esau to test Jacob's mettle: Is Jacob worthy of the blessing and to what lengths will he go to receive it? Such tests are fairly common in the Bible. One can only guess at the ways Isaac himself was traumatized when his father, Abraham, was put to the ultimate test and asked to sacrifice his only son (Gen. 22). And, let us not forget that Isaac concocted his own rather convincing hoodwinking when, just a chapter before, he dupes the Philistines into believing that Rebekah is his sister (Gen. 26).

Knowing full well that Rebekah would reveal the conversation between Isaac and Esau to Jacob, perhaps Isaac is a little wiser than he appears in the story. After all, what was supposed to be a deathbed blessing is not; Isaac is really nowhere near dying. In fact, he continues to live for many more years, enjoying the blessings of grandchildren, and his death is not recorded until a whopping seven chapters after the blessing debacle in Genesis 27. This new view of Isaac as a shrewd trickster lifts him from the shadowy figure who, quite frankly, seems otherwise unimpressive, and elevates him to a more patriarchal stance, making him a more appropriately matched mate for Rebekah. Let's face it: Only a strong man in his own right could handle the likes of her.

Whether or not Isaac is passively involved, or a trickster just like Rebekah and Jacob, is unclear. What we can say for certain is that Genesis 27 features Rebekah at her trickster best—using any means necessary to bring about God's plan as revealed to her in the oracle during her confinement. Once Rebekah accomplishes her mission and secures Jacob's rightful position as heir to the promise, she fades into the background and the stories of Jacob predominate.

The circumstances of her death are not recorded, but she is buried along with Abraham and Sarah, Isaac, Jacob and Leah, in the cave of Machpelah (Gen. 49:31), considered today to be a very holy site and, sadly, the scene of much violence. Because of her belief in Jacob as one who will continue the promise— and her dedication to the Lord—Rebekah is considered by many to be the most faithful of the biblical matriarchs.

Rebekah's Enduring Lessons

It is tempting to read Rebekah's story as pure entertainment— and, although her story is certainly that, it is much more. Remember that the biblical writers sought to teach us something; most often, something about God, but also something about ourselves, and the way we should treat others. So, what can we learn from Rebekah?

The first important lesson is that God's ways are mysterious. While Rebekah receives an oracle directly from God that essentially dictates the Divine Will, most of us are not so lucky. Throughout history, people have tried to understand what God wants from them, why God allows terrible things to happen to good people, and why some people, many of whom seem undeserving, seem to have all of the good things life has to offer. We try to make sense of the apparent inequalities in life through reason: Rich people work harder than poor people or bad things happen to us because we somehow deserve it. But these rationalizations usually fail to adequately explain life's disparities (i.e., usually rich people inherit money; how can we explain away the suffering of a child?). When there seems to be no logical explanation for the randomness that is life, we tend to shrug, shake our heads, and chalk things up to God's mysterious ways.

This notion of God's ways as mysterious is not only a recurring theme in the Bible, but also a particular theme throughout the stories of the patriarchs and matriarchs. For example, in reading about Israel's beginnings, we can't help but ask: Why does God choose to intervene in history at this particular time and with these particular people? And, more specifically, why does God choose Rebekah and why is Jacob slated as the continuation of the promise and not Esau, thus subverting the biblical tradition of primogeniture?

Scholars, teachers, and clergy have wrestled with these questions and have arrived at many attractive and plausible answers, but none are particularly satisfying. For example, when God's oracle to Rebekah asserts the supremacy of Jacob over Esau, no reason is given for this, nor does Rebekah question it. Some might argue that Esau, by his very nature—dull, physically repulsive, and almost animalistic—is an unsuitable candidate to continue the task of forming God's chosen people. While this argument seems reasonable, we must ask ourselves why God would set up such a cruel disparity between the brothers in the first place? What was the divine intention here?

Questions like these have fueled discussions between rabbis, theologians, and anyone else who has ever reflectively read this story. But, while the Bible instigates both pitched debate and prayerful reflection, it rarely—at least insofar as the great narratives of the Bible are concerned—gives us definitive answers. And so, we must continue to study, discuss, and ponder the meaning of a particular story. Perhaps God is found not so much in the answer, but in the unknown—in the mystery that is the question. The challenge, it seems, is to learn to be comfortable with the question.

Which brings us to the second important lesson Rebekah's tale can teach us. In the Bible—and usually in life—following God's will is, more often than not, difficult and challenging. Prophets, saints, mystics, and ordinary people have suffered much in the name of God. For this reason, many struggle against God. The Bible is filled with stories of women and men who find God's demands too daunting. Israel's great prophets, for the most part, find very little joy in their prophetic vocations.

We might also wonder if Rebekah, too, felt the burden of divine demands. We are not permitted to enter into her thoughts, but we do know that, from the moment God speaks to her revealing the destinies of her children, her life changes, and it does not seem to change for the better. Though she spent twenty years as a devoted and loving wife, she also endured the pain and heartache of barrenness which, in biblical antiquity, was considered a punishment from God and a source of shame.

There is often this "waiting period" associated with the Bible's barren woman stories. It is as if the woman must endure the trial of childlessness in order to grow as a person and to be worthy of mothering a powerful son. Sarah, Rebekah, Rachel, Hannah, and Samson's mother—just to name a few—endured this waiting period before giving birth to sons who were destined for greatness.

Still, despite her longing for a child, life is far less complicated for Rebekah before her sons are born. Once Jacob and Esau arrive, Rebekah must devote herself to not only raising and caring for two active sons, but also ever-present in her mind is the oracle. *She must make certain that the oracle is fulfilled.* On the surface, this appears to be an appropriate and faithful response, but faithful responses, as already mentioned, are usually not that simple. They often entail a great deal of self-sacrifice and suffering. While the Bible does not tell us that Rebekah herself suffered, it does tell us that her son Esau did.

Imagine Esau's pain, the feelings of inferiority and loneliness he must have felt living in the shadow of his brother all those years. Isaac and Rebekah do not attempt to hide the fact that they play favorites. We might assume that Isaac tries to compensate for Esau's lack of maternal nurturing, and today, we understand the psychological harm a child endures when rejected by his or her mother. Rebekah's favoritism, on the one hand, is necessary in order to ensure that Jacob becomes heir to the promise. On the other hand, her rejection of Esau seems cruel. For this and other reasons—not the least of which is her trickery—Rebekah has not always received a favorable review from the pulpit.

Of course, Isaac and Rebekah are not the only examples of poor parenting in the Bible. From Jephath's rash vow that result in his daughter's sacrificial death to David's coddling of his sons Amnon (who rapes his own sister) and Absalom (who mounts a rebellion against his father's kingship), the Bible is rife with stories of Parenting Gone Bad. Modern readers are often confused about how to read and interpret such stories.

To try to justify bad parenting by pointing to the chasm in time—after all, parents in biblical antiquity did not have access to parenting books and child psychologists to guide them—is only a partial explanation. We know that children in the Bible are received with much joy and considered God's greatest blessing. If children are so loved and cherished, why, then, are some—like Esau—treated so poorly? Of all those involved in the hoodwinking of Isaac, it is Esau who suffers most.

In order to try to make sense out of this, perhaps we need to examine the bad parenting stories from the author's perspective. In the case of Rebekah, maybe the author is trying to tell us—in the hit-you-over-the-head way that the Bible sometimes does—that Esau is not only unfit to assume the role as patriarch, but that he must, at all costs, be prevented from doing so. Moreover, this is part of God's plan as revealed to Rebekah. As mysterious as this plan may seem to us, it is clear that Rebekah understands her role in bringing the plan to fruition. The qualities Rebekah possesses—wit and cunning, confidence and courage—are the likely reasons why God singles her out for such a daunting task.

In any case, it is clear that doing God's will can cause division and alienation from those we love and we can end up hurting others. Contemporary readers may discern this division and alienation not only on a global level, with the bickering amongst, and even within, various religious groups, but also in a more personal way. When, for example, a family member converts to another religion or embraces a more orthodox or liberal version of the religion of their tribe, there is often irreparable harm done to prior relationships.

This final lesson reminds us that our actions affect others far beyond our immediate reckoning. While few of us can claim divine directives as an explanation for our actions—especially actions that are harmful or hurtful to another, as in Rebekah's trickery—we can nonetheless recognize that we rarely act in isolation. The very notion of community rests on this basic premise. The Bible has a consistent message regarding the sacredness of the community; that is, the integrity of the community must be maintained at all costs, for it is the very foundation of God's chosen people. Those who break the rules or otherwise undermine the community must be punished or removed. While this may seem to be harsh rhetoric for modern sensibilities, this truth is at the heart of every law in contemporary democracies.

Rebekah, the trickster, schemer, and questionable parent, plays a crucial role in Israel's history. As one of the founding mothers, she is involved in the formation of God's chosen people—a community of people who will transform the world and whose theology and ethics will lay the foundation for the three great monotheistic religions: Judaism, Christianity, and Islam. In this way, her actions can be viewed as part of a larger mural which contributes to a work far greater than anything she could have imagined.

Rahab: Lover, Liar, and Lawbreaker
The Hooker with a Heart of Gold

(Josh. 2; 6:16–25)

Before they went to sleep, she came up to them on the roof and said to the men: "I know that the Lord has given you the land, and that dread of you has fallen on us, and that all the inhabitants of the land melt in fear before you. For we have heard how the Lord dried up the water of the Red Sea before you when you came out of Egypt, and what you did to the two kings of the Amorites that were beyond the Jordan, to Sihon and Og, whom you utterly destroyed. As soon as we heard it, our hearts failed, and there was no courage left in any of us because of you. The Lord your God is indeed God in heaven above and on earth below. Now then, since I have dealt kindly with you, swear to me by the Lord that you in turn will deal kindly with my family. Give me a sign of good faith that you will spare my father and mother, my brothers and sisters, and all who belong to them, and deliver our lives from death." The men said to her, "Our life for yours! If you do not tell this business of ours, then we will deal kindly and faithfully with you when the Lord gives us the land."

Then she let them down by a rope through the window, for her house was on the outer side of the city wall and she resided within the wall itself (Josh. 2:8–15).

FROM BIANCA in Shakespeare's *Othello* to Vivian (played by Julia Roberts) in the 1990 film *Pretty Woman*, the hooker with a heart of gold is a common stock character in literature, poetry, and film. Rahab, the Bible's version of a good girl gone bad gone good, is the courageous courtesan who flings open the gates of the Promised Land for the children of Israel, thus fulfilling God's promise to Abraham (Gen. 12:1–4). But Rahab is more than just a kindhearted working girl. Indeed, she stands at the threshold of a new era for the people of Israel, and her life, actions, and faith in Yhwh place her at the forefront of the Bible's great heroic figures.

Rahab's story begins as the epic adventure of Israel's exodus from Egypt and forty-year sojourn in the wilderness draws to a close. After the death of Moses, a new leader, Joshua, leads the Israelites, under the banner of divine inheritance, to the edge of the Promised Land. But, there seems to be a slight problem: Apparently, there are people already living in the land originally deeded to Abraham (Gen. 12:6–7). Granted, it has taken a few hundred years for God's promise to materialize, but, at least according to the Bible, this land belongs to the Israelites, which means that the current inhabitants must go.

The actual manner in which the Israelites acquire the land—thus driving out the Canaanite inhabitants—is the subject of much debate. Some scholars point to the archeological record that suggests a gradual infiltration into the land while others advocate the considerable evidence that indicates the numerous battles and horrific bloodshed involved in Israel's confrontations with the various tribes of Canaan—a theory closer to the version presented in the book of Joshua. It seems likely that the truth is somewhere in between these two theories.

In any case, according to the book of Joshua, the immediate problem is how to wrestle the land from the Canaanites, whom the Israelites view as mere squatters. Joshua decides to send a couple of spies to assess the situation. Astute readers of the Bible will note that this is not the first time spies are sent out to reconnoiter this land. In Numbers 13, Moses sends out spies who return in fear, reporting that giants (*anakim*) dwell in the Promised Land. Of course, there are no giants; only the Canaanites with their massive walled cites. Perhaps the spies assume such impressive structures are the work of giants? Understandably, the decision is made at that time to delay entry into the land; after all, timing is everything. It takes many more years for God to form the chosen people into the fierce warriors now led by Joshua.

Upon entering the city of Jericho, Joshua's spies head immediately to the local whorehouse (Josh. 2:1). The story does not tell us why the men decide to make a pit stop at the bordello. Perhaps those forty years of wandering in the wilderness had something to do with it, or maybe they sought to gather secret information about the city from the working girls sometimes coaxed from clients in the throes of passion. Whatever their reasons, the stop seems fortuitous, for it is here that they encounter the madam, Rahab, who becomes their protector, confidant, and friend.

The spies decide to spend the night at Rahab's house and someone—perhaps another patron—reports their presence in the city to the king of Jericho. Clearly uncomfortable with foreign spies in his town (for he is aware of their covert mission, Josh. 2:2), the king orders Rahab to turn over the men to the authorities (Josh. 2:3).

We must pause for a moment to consider Rahab's present position. She is a Canaanite and so we might naturally assume that her loyalties are to her king and her people. In fact, had we not known the ending of this particular story, we might even suspect that Rahab herself might be the aforementioned informant to the king. As a single woman and prostitute, she is marginalized and powerless, even within the more socially liberal Canaanite culture. It therefore makes good business sense for Rahab to remain on good terms with the king and local authorities, and ratting on the spies will certainly keep her in their good graces. But as we will soon see, Rahab's motives stem from an interest in an authority far greater than any earthly king.

Rahab disregards the king's injunction to turn over Israel's scouts, and instead hides them safely on her roof, under stalks of drying flax. When questioned, she lies easily to the king's henchmen, an occupational requirement in her particular business, not just once but four times, sending them away from the city on a wild goose chase.

> "True, the men came to me, but I did not know where they came from. And when it was time to close the gate at dark, the men went out. Where the men went, I do not know. Pursue them quickly, for you can overtake them" (Josh. 2:5).

While she admits that there were indeed spies in her bordello, she lies about their identity, and fabricates a story of escape in which she makes it seem plausible that the spies may still be captured. The king's men seem convinced and depart to search in vain for the spies who, ironically, remain ensconced on Rahab's roof.

Initially, it may seem confusing as to why Rahab would risk her life and livelihood for Joshua's spies, but she soon reveals her motives. When the coast is clear, Rahab returns to the roof and speaks to Joshua's men. It appears that Israel's reputation as fierce warriors and divine destiny is well-known among the local population, including Rahab: "I know that the Lord has given you the land, and that dread of you has fallen on us, and that all the inhabitants of the land melt in fear of you" (Josh. 2:9). Rahab also mentions Israel's stunning victories over the Egyptians and the Amorites (Josh. 2:10) and she admits that she—and her people—fear the powerful Israelites.

But unlike the locals, who likely view Israel as the current tribal bully du jour with whom they must reckon, Rahab somehow understands Israel's muscle as divine in origin, so much so that this not-so-good Canaanite girl professes belief in the God of Israel: "The Lord, your God is indeed God in heaven above and on earth below" (Josh. 2:11). It all makes sense now: her courage in defying the king and rescuing the spies is the result of her newfound faith in the God of Israel, who fortifies and strengthens her, just as he fortifies and strengthens his chosen people. Moreover, it is Rahab's confession of faith that places her squarely on the Bible's list of good girls as she represents the first convert in the Promised Land. That she is a woman, a foreigner, and a prostitute makes her conversion all the more astounding.

Of course, a careful reading of the text raises a few questions, specifically: Are there ulterior motives involved in Rahab's conversion experience and her allegiance to the spies and, ostensibly, to the Israelites and their God? We do not know that the spies believe Rahab's profession of faith is genuine, for harlots often lie to get what they want. And, as Rahab continues her conversation with the spies, she asks for recompense for her loyalty, which certainly gives us pause to consider that perhaps there are other motives at work:

> "Now then, since I have dealt kindly with you, swear to me by the Lord that you in turn will deal kindly with my family. Give me a sign of good faith that you will spare my father and mother, my brothers and sisters, and all who belong to them, and deliver our lives from death" (Josh. 2:12–13).

Prostitutes do not give away their services for free; in exchange for services rendered, Rahab asks the spies to spare her and her family when the Israelites attack Jericho. The spies agree, but they have a few strings attached of their own: Rahab must keep their mission a secret (Josh. 2:14, 20) and they are still in need of her assistance in order to escape Jericho. Madams are nothing if not discreet; the spies can rest assured that their espionage activities will be held in the strictest of confidence. Rahab then helps the men to leave the city by lowering a rope and easing them out of her window, "for her house was on the outer side of the city wall and she resided within the wall itself" (Josh. 2:15).

As the men depart, Rahab instructs them to hide in the hill country for three days so that the king's men will not find them. In return, the spies give Rahab a crimson cord to tie to her window, thus marking her house and those inside for preservation when the Israelites invade the city. They further warn her to make certain that her family remains inside, or else they will be subjected to the sword (Josh. 2:18–19). As the spies depart, Rahab ties the red cord to her window, an action evocative of the Passover story in which the Israelites are saved from destruction by marking their doors with the blood of the paschal lamb (Exod. 12:21–23).

The men follow Rahab's advice and lay low in the hills for three days before they return to Joshua. Using Rahab's own words, the spies tell Joshua that the land is ripe for the taking and that "all the inhabitants of the land melt in fear before us" (Josh. 2:24).

The invasion of Jericho (Josh. 6) is often described as a "liturgical battle" for it involves the whole of Israel, including her priests, and has elements normally reserved for Israelite religious services, such as the presence of the ark of the covenant and the sounding of the *shofar* horn. In anticipation of the invasion, the city has been heavily fortified; the city gate is closed and the residents remain shut up in their houses, bracing themselves for the inevitable onslaught of Joshua and his army. But before we explore the battle itself, it seems wise to first say a few words about the mode of ancient warfare used at this time known as the *ban*.

It is interesting to note that in recent years, much has been made of the so-called holy war texts in the *Qur'an*, yet most Jews and Christians are surprised to learn that the Bible has a few holy war references of its own, including the story of the destruction of Jericho in Joshua 6. To be sure, we are not

talking about some invented biblical machismo or ancient
Israelite chest pounding here, for there is ample archeological
and extrabiblical evidence that supports the veracity of the
Bible's holy war tradition.

Called the *ban* in the Bible (in Hebrew, *herem),* the dictates of this holy war are chilling and terrifying. It requires the
Israelites to utterly destroy the enemy, killing anyone who lives
in the city, including infants, pregnant women, old people and
even animals. Following what can only be described as a
bloodbath, the city is then set ablaze and burned to the
ground. Nothing may be taken; there are no spoils for the victor, other than precious metals, which are to be taken and
placed in the treasury of the Lord. Understandably, this sce-
nario is hard for modern readers to take. Harder still is the fact
that mastermind behind the butchery of the ban is none other
than Yhwh. And, because the battle is for the glory of the
Lord, it must be executed with ruthless precision; failure to do
so provokes divine punishment.

Rahab knows well the misery of the ban; she has likely
heard soldiers who frequent her bordello brag about it and, in
the barbarous world of the ancient Near East, may have even
witnessed its devastation. It comes as no surprise, then, that
Rahab will do just about anything to rescue her family from the
Israelite sword. Her deal with the spies, however, is specious.
Will they honor their vow and spare Rahab and her family? Or
will they renege on their promise, or worse, forget about it?

As the Israelites storm the city in a frontal attack, putting
to the sword "all in the city, both men and women, young and
old, oxen, sheep, and donkeys" (Josh. 6:21), the tension builds.
And then, amidst the screams and bloodshed, there is an
almost audible sigh of relief as Joshua remembers Rahab and
her family.

He commands the two spies to honor their oath and to rescue the courageous prostitute and her kin. Just as Rahab rescued the spies and brought them safely outside the city walls,
the spies now rescue Rahab and her family and situate them

outside the city and away from the final destruction. "They burned down the city, and everything in it . . . But Rahab the prostitute, with her family and all who belonged to her, Joshua spared" (Josh. 6:25). The story ends on a happily-ever-after note: "Her family has lived in Israel ever since. For she hid the messengers whom Joshua sent to spy out Jericho" (Josh. 6:25).

Rahab, the unlikely heroine who heralds Israel's occupation of the land, reminds us of Rebekah (Gen. 24–27) and Tamar (Gen. 38), sister tricksters, whose resourcefulness and cleverness help to bring about God's plan. While it is clear that Rahab's bag of tricks helps to bring about God's plan for Israel in their conquest of the Promised Land, her story carries a critical collateral message: Faith in Yhwh saves. It is Rahab's faith in the God who saves that makes her one of the most memorable women in the Hebrew Bible.

Rahab's Enduring Lessons

Rahab's story is inspirational in many ways. Her courage, strength, and self-sacrificing love are common elements found in heroine or hero tales in the Bible and in literature. But what makes Rahab's heroine story so unique is her unusual devotion to another people's God and the manner in which her faith transforms her—these are the most enduring lessons of her story.

Women in biblical antiquity are presented as peripheral creatures, hovering on the sidelines of a society dominated by men. Foreign women, in particular, are distrusted, not so much because they are foreign, but because their religious beliefs pollute the pure waters of Yahwistic faith. And prostitutes, then and now, represent the underbelly of society and are viewed with disdain and disgust. Rahab begins with these three strikes against her: she's a woman, a foreigner, and a prostitute, hardly the sort of heroine one might expect.

Let us not forget, however, that the God of Israel has a demonstrated soft spot for the underdog. Indeed, God rarely favors the biggest, best, or brightest, and those specifically called to the Lord's friendship are usually flawed, some hope-lessly. Rahab's blemished life is obvious; the biblical author does not attempt to cover the fact that she is a harlot. But, in many ways, Rahab also represents Israel, the undisputed underdog of the ancient Near East. Their recent history includes Egyptian enslavement, liberation by an unlikely hero (Moses), and attacks from fierce enemies during their wander-ings in the wilderness. Still, they emerge the victors because they have Yhwh on their side, fighting for them and protect-ing them. It comes as no surprise, then, that God should choose the underdog, Rahab; that *she chooses God*, however, is what makes her story so exceptional.

If her actions in ignoring the king's demands, lying to the king's soldiers, hiding and helping Joshua's spies to escape are risky, they are nothing compared to the risk she undertakes in vowing allegiance to the transcendent God of the Israelites. Rahab's faith-inspired actions represent biblical heroism at its best. Indeed, her chutzpah and courage represent only part of her appeal; it is her *faith* that the biblical writer(s) sought to emphasize.

Rahab's faith gives us pause to question our own faith and to ponder the meaning of religious faith in general. Faith, after all, cannot be proven; it is intangible, intuitive, and in many ways, irrational. The profession of faith is largely a calculated risk; it cannot be subjected to scientific analysis and we have no way of knowing for certain if we are right. And so, like Rahab, we hedge our bets, cross our fingers, and jump in with both feet. Rahab does not know for certain that God's chosen people will save her and her family, but she's betting on it.

Her saving actions are heroic, yes, but that they are inspired by *faith* gives us an occasion to turn inward and to ask ourselves how much of what we do is inspired by faith? For most of us, daily living is consumed with mindless tasks and the requisite demands of work and family. We tend to pigeonhole our faith life into holy days, temple/church rituals, or the occasional crisis that evokes panicked cries to the heavens for rescue. In short, we often view faith as a noun rather than a verb, as something apart from ordinary life, to be taken out and dusted off once a week. How different would life be if faith inspired our actions? Believers often claim that faith helps to counter the fear, doubt, anxiety, and indecision that have become the hallmarks of modern life, a claim perhaps worth testing.

But, in addition to her faith-inspired heroism, Rahab's story is also a story of transformation. Like the new and fortified Israel, whose faith and courage is borne from the years of captivity, the uncertainty of the wilderness, and the battles with adversaries, Rahab, too, is changed by her newfound faith.

It is her faith that gives her strength to act, to defy her king, lie to his men, broker a deal with the spies, and to trust that they will honor their promise to her. Of course, her story of transformation is a familiar one: The tart with a heart finds a savior who changes her life. But Rahab's story of transformation is also unique, for she is saved, but also saves; she rescues the spies, who then rescue her. This places her on equal footing with the men in the story and accents her inner strength and courage, all highly unusual for a woman in the smothering, sexually repressive world of biblical antiquity. We are also reminded that sometimes saviors emerge among unlikely people and in unlikely places. And, we need to be open to the saviors around us, for they often do not come from the ranks of trusted friends and family.

Finally, Rahab's transformation highlights a common biblical theme: Through God, all things are possible. Her story, then, offers hope for the rest of us underdogs. If God can transform Rahab, the Canaanite prostitute, there is hope for us, too.

3

Delilah: Lover
Tricks or Tryst?

(Judg. 16)

Then she said to him, "How can you say, 'I love you,' when your heart is not with me? You have mocked me three times now and have not told me what makes your strength so great." Finally, after she had nagged him with her words day after day, and pestered him, he was tired to death. So he told her his whole secret, and said to her, "A razor has never come upon my head; for I have been a nazirite to God from my mother's womb. If my head were shaved, then my strength would leave me; I would become weak, and be like anyone else."

When Delilah realized that he had told her his whole secret, she sent and called the lords of the Philistines, saying, "This time come up, for he has told his whole secret to me." Then the lords of the Philistines came up to her, and brought the money in their hands. She let him fall asleep on her lap; and she called a man, and had him shave off the seven locks of his head. He began to weaken, and his strength left him. Then she said, "The Philistines are upon you, Samson!" (Judg. 16:15–20).

K NOWN AS THE deceitful courtesan who coaxes from
Samson the secret of his superhuman strength only to
betray him to enemies, Delilah is of one of the Bible's
most notorious bad girls. But, like all the women stories in the
Bible, there is more to her story than the popular rendition of
it handed down to us through the ages. To better understand
the *real* story of Delilah, her actions must be viewed in the context of the greater narrative about Samson, her oversexed paramour and the unlikely victim who falls into her snare.

Samson is the biblical version of a superhero, a man
blessed with great physical power who has been consecrated
as one of the Lord's chosen to deliver Israel from the clutches
of the Philistines. Like all superheroes, Samson's conception
and birth are miraculous. His birth to an unnamed, barren
mother is a common motif in the Bible and reminds us of
Sarah (Gen. 21:1–7) and other barren women, including
Rebekah, Rachel, Hannah, and the Shunammite Woman.
While the barren woman stories may differ slightly, the outcome is always the same: The child born (always male) is destined for greatness and Samson, whose conception and birth
is preceded by angelic announcement to his mother, is no
exception:

> "Although you are barren, having borne no children, you
> shall conceive and bear a son. Now be careful not to
> drink wine or strong drink, or to eat anything unclean,
> for you shall conceive and bear a son. No razor is to
> come to his head, for the boy shall be a nazirite to God
> from birth. It is he who shall begin to deliver Israel from
> the hand of the Philistines" (Judg. 13:4–5).

According to the angel, Samson will be a special child who
will *begin* the process of delivering Israel from the Philistines.
Special Samson is consecrated a *nazirite* (from the Hebrew
word for "consecrated") from the womb and is thus prohib-
ited from drinking alcohol, consuming ritually unclean food,

touching dead bodies, and cutting his hair. Nazirites are sacred volunteers, dedicated to serving the Lord, and although the nazirite vow (Num. 6:1–11) is normally taken for a brief period of time, there are a few men, such as Samson, Samuel, and John the Baptist, who take this vow for a lifetime. Although men or women may take this vow, there is no record in the Bible of a female nazirite. All of this makes Samson seem awfully holy, but the truth is, Samson will set out to break nearly all of his nazirite vows.

The coveted only child of previously barren parents, Samson is probably pampered and often reminded of his specialness. Perhaps it is Samson's notion of himself as "special" that governs much of his later behavior, since coddled children rarely grow into altruistic adults. Still, our expectations of Samson are high. Surely he will use his special gifts to ransom Israel from those pesky Philistines. Unfortunately, Samson uses his gifts not to benefit his people, but for personal gain. Israel's great hope turns out to be a great disappointment, for Samson is governed less by his nazirite status to serve Yhwh than he is dominated by his sexual appetite for foreign women.

Three times Samson crosses over into Philistine territory in search of female companionship, but if ever a man was unlucky in love, it is Samson. Samson first fancies and then marries a Philistine woman from Timnah. On his way to visit his soon-to-be bride, Samson is attacked by a lion, which he kills barehanded (Judg. 14:6). Later, he finds a stash of honey in the lion's carcass and eats some. Eating the honey from the lion's carcass is in violation of his nazirite vows, but Samson does not seem to concern himself with such details, for he takes whatever he wants. He also uses the occasion to construct a riddle for his wedding guests: "Out of the eater came something to eat. Out of the strong came something sweet" (Judg. 14:14). Whoever can answer the riddle will receive thirty new garments.

Of course, no one but Samson can possibly answer the riddle. The frustrated wedding guests threaten to murder Samson's new bride and her family unless she provides them with the answer to Samson's unanswerable riddle. Out of fear, and in order to protect her family, she pesters Samson until he answers the riddle and she promptly betrays him to "her people" (Judg. 14:17).

When Samson finds out, he murders thirty innocent people in a fit of rage and gives their garments to pay off the Philistine party guests. Thinking her abandoned, his father-in-law gives Samson's wife to his best man, which triggers another violent episode: Samson sets certain Philistine fields ablaze, and the Philistines respond by burning to death Samson's former wife and her father (Judg. 15:3–6). Samson slaughters the perpetrators and later, with jawbone of an ass, slays a thousand other Philistines who come out to apprehend him (Judg. 15:15).

Samson has now become the Philistines' Public Enemy Number One and they desperately want to capture him before he does more harm. If Samson had any sense, he might consider laying low until things calm down. But, Samson has an itch that only a Philistine prostitute can scratch. Daring to return to the scene of the crime, Samson arranges a tête-à-tête with a Philistine harlot from Gaza who knows about his violent past and tips off her countrymen (Judg. 16:1–2). Hoping to capture him in the wee hours of the morning as he leaves the prostitute, they lie in wait for him. But Samson outsmarts them and, sneaking out before sun up, rips the massive city gates from their hinges and carries them off on his back (Judg. 16:4).

Samson is a wild man, prone to outbursts of violence, who races along the corridor of forbidden cities, courting forbidden women, his long hair flying behind him as he wreaks havoc upon the locals who fear him. But one woman, Delilah, will put an end to all that rowdiness. From Enkidu, domesticated by the prostitute Shamhat in the ancient Mesopotamian tale *The Epic of Gilgamesh*, to more modern renditions, including Tarzan and Jane or the beauty and the beast, Samson joins the ranks of other hirsute wild men in literature who are tamed by women.

The last in the triad of foreign women to betray Samson, Delilah alone is named. We do not know how long the relationship between Delilah and Samson lasted, nor the nature of their relationship, though most scholars speculate it was a sexual one. What is certain is that Samson falls in love with Delilah and she, in a sense, tames him.

Delilah is from the valley of Sorek, an area of mixed ethnicities, and though she is never identified in the text as a Philistine, her actions in the story seem to indicate as much (Judg. 16:4). Moreover, given Samson's predilection for Philistine females, it seems likely that Delilah is herself Philistine. Though traditionally branded a prostitute, nowhere in the story does it state Delilah's profession. We know only that she is a woman who lives alone, without a man to take care of her. Some scholars speculate that she is a weaver of cloth because the text mentions a weaving pin, loom, and Delilah's ability to weave Samson's hair (Judg. 16:14). Since most women in biblical antiquity are in charge of making and mending clothes, this evidence alone cannot definitively point to her profession, which must remain a mystery.

Like Rahab, she manages her own life; but also like Rahab, she must navigate through the complicated social maze of the male-dominated society in which she lives. This makes her vulnerable and a target for the Philistine elders who offer to pay her handsomely if she can uncover the secret of Samson's great strength (Judg. 16:5). But perhaps the most important detail in Delilah's story is the fact that Samson is in love with her (Judg. 16:4). This crucial fact allows the scene to unfold to its sad end.

Though Delilah is traditionally depicted as a liar, it is Samson, not Delilah, who consistently fails to tell the truth. Delilah does not use her feminine wiles to coax an answer, but asks Samson directly about the source of his strength: "Please, tell me what makes your strength so great, and how you could be bound, so that one could subdue you" (Judg. 16:4). Perhaps Samson is under the impression that Delilah has some sort of sexual bondage game in mind, for he tells her that binding him with seven green bowstrings would make him weak. As the Philistine lords wait just outside the door, Delilah, apparently with Samson's consent and knowledge binds him with the seven green bowstrings. When she exclaims: "The Philistines are upon you, Samson" (Judg. 16:9), he easily snaps the strings.

Delilah accuses Samson of mocking her and again asks him the source of his strength. He replies: "If they bind me with new ropes that have not been used, then I shall become weak, and be like anyone else" (Judg. 16:11). Once again, Delilah ties up Samson and once again he breaks free. Undeterred, Delilah asks again and this time Samson moves closer to the truth and tells her that if his hair is woven and bound, he will become weak like any other person.

Delilah waits for him to fall asleep and then weaves his hair into a web. When she wakes him with the threat of the Philistines, Samson shakes his hair free from the web. Though Samson seems to view all of this as some sort of lovers' game or sexual banter, Delilah does not. She has a job to do and must switch tactics. A woman knows when a man is in love with her and Delilah is no fool. Using his love for her to her advantage and taking things up a notch, Delilah first accuses Samson of not loving her and when this fails, she simply nags him until he finally reveals his secret: "A razor has never come upon my head; for I have been a nazirite for God from my mother's womb. If my head were shaved, my strength would leave me" (Judg. 16:17).

Convinced that Samson has finally revealed the true source of his strength, Delilah summons the Philistine lords and waits for the opportune moment to betray him. In a painfully poignant scene, Samson, exhausted from all that nagging, sleeps peacefully on the lap of his lover, unaware of his impending betrayal. In his slumber, Delilah has "a man" shave the seven locks of hair from Samson's head. As the locks are shorn, Samson's strength leaves him and the Philistines, at last, have their man (Judg. 16:19).

Samson's captors bind him and gouge out his eyes. The man so blinded by his love for Delilah is now physically without sight. In Philistine custody, he spends the rest of his days "grinding." While most translations indicate that Samson was treated like an animal and forced to grind grain at a mill, some scholars speculate that Samson was forced to do grinding of a different sort. That is, because of his superior strength, Samson was essentially put out to stud. In later Philistine tales, such as the story of David and Goliath (1 Sam. 17), some Philistines seem to have superhuman strength, perhaps because they share an ancestry with the great Samson. In either case, ever so slowly, apparently without the Philistines taking notice, Samson's hair begins to grow back, and with it, his strength (Judg. 16:22).

In the last episode of this tragic tale, Samson is bound between the pillars of the Philistine temple dedicated to their god, Dagon. Samson prays to the God of Israel for strength. God hears his prayer and Samson, exacting a final dose of terror upon the Philistines, pulls in the pillars causing the temple to collapse upon the Philistine worshippers, and also upon himself (Judg. 16:28–30). In this final act of redemption, Samson fulfills his mission as the one who will "*begin* to deliver Israel from the hand of the Philistines" (Judg. 13:5).

Although Delilah fades from the story after Samson's capture, the question, "Why, why, why, Delilah?" lingers. Why does she betray the man who loves her? Is it for the money, or is she just patently evil? Could it be that the whole episode is a setup, an elaborate trap orchestrated by the Philistine lords, and that Delilah is in cahoots with them? Or, is she just a helpless pawn, a victim who has perhaps heard about what happens to women like Samson's wife who fail to comply with the demands of the Philistine men?

While money seems to be Delilah's primary motivation (after all, a woman on her own must be practical), it seems likely Delilah had another reason for betraying Samson. The chapters preceding Samson's dalliance with Delilah narrate his reign of terror throughout the Philistine territory. Perhaps Delilah, like the rest of her countrymen and women, is fed up with Samson's terrorist activities and decides, once and for all, to put an end to his murderous rampages. Whatever her motivation, at the very least, Delilah's betrayal of Samson seals his fate and sets into motion the deliverance of God's chosen people from the hand of the Philistines.

Delilah's Enduring Lessons

What can we possibly learn from a bad girl like Delilah? Beyond the author's obvious lesson regarding the dangers of foreign women, are the tandem lessons of loyalty and betrayal. Though Delilah's story is rarely viewed as a lesson in loyalty, it is her allegiance to her own people that, at least in part, motivates her to seek the source of Samson's superhuman strength and to then betray him. Perhaps the best way to understand Delilah's particular brand of loyalty is to contrast her actions with two other biblical women, Rahab and Ruth.

Sandwiched between the books of Joshua and Ruth, the book of Judges tells the story of Israel's early occupation of the land under a loose tribal federation led by judges, like Samson. In Joshua and in Ruth, we are introduced to two foreign women, Rahab and Ruth, who behave in a manner acceptable to Israel. Both forsake their own people and profess faith in Yhwh and Israel. Rahab and Ruth are models of fidelity and devotion and, accordingly, both women receive positive reviews from the biblical editors. Never mind the fact that Rahab's betrayal of her own people results in their slaughter and that Ruth, a veritable biblical goody-two-shoes, abandons her family, home, and nation.

Delilah, on the other hand, remains loyal to her people, to the point of taking her life in her hands in order to rid the land of a dangerous menace. If today a woman single-handedly

brought about the arrest of a car bomber or any other terrorist, she would be hailed a heroine. Moreover, if Delilah's story
were told from a Philistine perspective, she would be considered a deliverer. Conversely, if we skew the stories of Rahab
and Ruth ever so slightly, both could be considered traitors.
And so, it is a matter of perspective.

On a larger scale, Delilah and the other two nameless
Philistine women in Samson's life demonstrate how Israel
ought to behave. The triad of betrayals, culminating in
Delilah's, is narrated without judgment, perhaps as a way to
contrast Philistine national fidelity with Israelite infidelity, a
persistent problem in the Bible. Indeed, Israel's fickle love affair
with Yhwh is the topic of later prophetic warnings ("Repent
and turn away from all your transgressions..." Ezek. 18:30),
Torah injunctions ("You shall have no other gods..." Exod.
20:3), and countless divine reprimands ("I will punish you for
all your iniquities..." Amos 3:2). But despite the constant
reminders to honor the covenant and to remain faithful to the
One God, the chosen people choose not to get the message.

The trio of Philistine females associated with Samson,
however, understands the meaning of loyalty; betraying Samson is viewed as their civic responsibility. Not so with adulter-
ess Israel. She chases after other gods and forsakes the Lord.
Even Samson's own people, recognizing him to be a public
menace, attempt to turn him over to Philistine authorities, but
he slaughters his would-be captors (Judg. 15:9–17). This is not
the proper way Israel should respond to the Lord's chosen
judge, even if he is more of a schoolyard bully than a deliverer.

And, while the biblical author does not excuse Delilah's
behavior, neither is she condemned. Though it is tempting to
imagine the author's tacit approval of her actions, we cannot
help but hear the quiet caution whispered through the sands
of time: "Be careful who you trust." And foreign women are
forbidden for good reason. They worship gods other than
Yhwh and can turn the hearts of Israelite men away from the

Lord. Samson's biggest mistake is trusting Delilah. But trust is the essence of love, for without it, love dies.

Delilah's betrayal is made easier by the fact that Samson loves her; of course, it is important to note that nowhere in the text does it state that she loves him. This alone makes the story a tragedy, for unrequited love is always heartbreaking. It would be a mistake, however, to say that Samson's ultimate fate is the result of Delilah's betrayal. Samson, after all, paves the way to his binding between the pillars with violence and mayhem. Her betrayal aside, we cannot help but wonder how it is that Samson, the Testosterone Terminator, earns the reputation of one of the Bible's great heroes in the first place.

Finally, Delilah's actions are motivated, at least in part, by self-preservation. In the male-dominated world of biblical antiquity, a woman alone must do what she must to survive: Rebekah tricks Isaac; Rahab lies about the Israelite spies; and Delilah betrays Samson. Trickery, lies, and betrayal, it seems, are the tools of the trade for many biblical women, who must sometimes use less than reputable means to advance their cause. Understood in this way, Delilah's story speaks to contemporary women everywhere who struggle to carve out a life for themselves and often their children in what is still very much a man's world. Women still receive less pay and promotional opportunities than their male counterparts and like it or not, the lion's share of childcare and other domestic duties are still borne by women. While we may eschew her tactics, we nonetheless understand them within the context of the patriarchal society in which she lives. In short, if the elders demand that Delilah ensnare Samson, it is in her best interest to comply.

Her lessons and legacy are therefore a mixed bag. And, despite her tarnished reputation as the woman who brought about Samson's downfall, Delilah is a survivor who ultimately rescues her people from a deadly scourge.

Ruth: Lover
The Girl Next Door

(Ruth 1–4)

So she set out from the place where she had been living, she and her two daughters-in-law, and they went on their way to go back to the land of Judah. But Naomi said to her two daughters-in-law, "Go back each of you to your mother's house. May the Lord deal kindly with you, as you have dealt with the dead and with me. The Lord grant that you may find security, each of you in the house of your husband." Then she kissed them, and they wept aloud. They said to her, "No, we will return with you to your people." But Naomi said, "Turn back, my daughters, why will you go with me? Do I still have sons in my womb that they may become your husbands? Turn back, my daughters, go your way, for I am too old to have a husband. Even if I thought there was hope for me, even if I should have a husband tonight and bear sons, would you then wait until they were grown? Would you then refrain from marrying? No, my daughters, it has been far more bitter for me than for you, because the hand of the Lord has turned against me." Then they wept aloud again. Orpah kissed her mother-in-law, but Ruth clung to her.

So she said, "See, your sister-in-law has gone back to her people and to her gods; return after your sister-in-law." But Ruth said, "Do not press me to leave you or to turn back from following you! Where you go, I will go; where you lodge, I will lodge; your people shall be my people, and your God my God. Where you die, I will die—there will I be buried. May the Lord do thus and so to me, and more as well, if even death parts me from you!" When Naomi saw that she was determined to go with her, she said no more to her (Ruth 1:7–18).

THE MODEL of filial devotion, loyalty, and friendship, Ruth is the biblical version of the girl next door, the cheerleader with the straight white teeth, and the Girl Scout who helps old ladies cross the street. This image of perfection may seem surprising given the fact that Ruth is a Moabite, a suspicious foreigner from across the Jordan River. She may be from the wrong side of the river, but her ethnic origins cannot detract from her stellar reputation as Bible's quintessential good girl who does all the right things. In fact, the book named after her is perhaps the only book in the Bible where *all* the characters do the right thing. Of course, it would be a mistake to view Ruth as a one-dimensional character. Indeed, beneath the veneer of perfection is a displaced woman who shoulders the responsibility of caring for her mother-in-law in the midst of her own personal sorrow.

Ruth begins almost like a "once upon a time" children's tale: "In the days when judges ruled" (Ruth 1:1). This is an indication that the setting of the story differs from the author's contemporary situation, a little detail to keep in mind in discerning the author's intention. There is considerable scholarly debate regarding the date of Ruth, but most scholars lean toward a post-exilic composition (anywhere from the sixth to the fifth century B.C.E.). This date makes a great deal of sense, given the fact that the people of Israel, fresh from their sojourn in Babylonia, are in the midst of some fairly rigorous religious and social reforms, one of which prohibits intermarriage (Ezra 9–10; Neh. 10:30). Ruth, then, may have been written as a way to counter such xenophobic laws, in effect, stating that even foreigners can become part of the community of the Lord.

Ruth reads almost like a play, with changing scenes and memorable characters that weave theological strands of meaning into the plot. Scene one, the Prologue (Ruth 1:1–5) reveals a desperate situation. Naomi's husband, Elimelech, and their two sons, Mahlon and Chilion, leave their home in the famine-stricken Bethlehem and settle in Moab. Descendents

from the incestuous union between Lot and his eldest daughter (Gen. 19:37), the Moabites are the occasional enemies of
the Israelites, known for their apostasy and sexual immoral-
ity. The text makes no mention of these juicy tidbits, however, and Naomi and her family live peacefully in Moab for
ten years. At some point, Elimelech dies and eventually both
boys marry local Moabite girls. Mahlon marries Ruth and
Chilion marries Orpah (not Oprah!) and sometime after,
Naomi's sons also die, leaving their widows childless. The Prologue thus sets the theme of barrenness in the form of famine,
death, and childlessness, which may be a subtle commentary
on the dangers of living in a foreign land and inbreeding with
the locals.

In the second scene (Ruth 1:6–22), realizing their vulnera-
bility and learning that the famine in Bethlehem is now over,
Naomi makes the decision to return to her homeland and her
people. Ruth and Orpah set out with her, but Orpah turns
back and remains with her family in Moab. Despite Naomi's
persistent urgings to also remain in Moab with her family,
Ruth refuses to abandon her mother-in-law. Ruth's loyalty to
her mother-in-law, so beautifully and eloquently stated, is often
part of contemporary wedding vows:

> "Do not press me to leave you
> or to turn back from following
> you!
> Where you go, I will go;
> Where you lodge, I will lodge;
> Your people shall be my people;
> And your God, my God.
> Where you die, I will die—
> There I will be buried.
> May the Lord do thus and so
> To me,
> And more as well,
> If even death parts me from you" (Ruth 1:16–17).

Ruth's powerful confession of love and devotion—both to her mother-in-law and to Naomi's God—makes her the poster child for foreign wives in Israel. Like Rahab (Josh. 2:11), Ruth professes faith in Yhwh, which means she's a convert and therefore an acceptable candidate for a wife. Indeed, Ruth's appeal is not so much her allegiance to Naomi, but to Naomi's God. Still, any woman who has a mother-in-law has to marvel at Ruth's relationship with Naomi—whose self-designated moniker is "Mara" (bitter). Naomi is bitter because of her situation and blames God for her present predicament. If there is a conflict in this everyone-does-the-right-thing story, it is between Naomi and God. Ruth undoubtedly gets an earful of Naomi's bitterness, yet she remains by her side and becomes the unfortunate yardstick by which all future daughters-in-law are measured (and by which most fall short).

Together, bitter Naomi and dutiful Ruth return to Bethlehem to an uncertain future. The author offers a glimmer of hope, however, at the close of this otherwise dismal scene: "They came to Bethlehem at the beginning of the barley harvest" (Ruth 1:22). From barrenness and death, is the hope of abundance and new life.

Scene three (Ruth 2:1–23) opens with an immediate problem for the two widows: how to get food. The ever-resourceful Ruth who, even as a foreigner, is somehow aware of the Israelite law that commands farmers to leave behind some of their harvest for the poor (Lev. 19:9–10; 23:22; Deut. 24:19–22), sets out to procure some grain. As Ruth works behind the harvesters in the field, she has a chance encounter with a man named Boaz, a rich relative of Elimelech, and the owner of the field. Boaz asks his servants about her and is told: "She is the Moabite who came back with Naomi from the country of Moab" (Ruth 2:6). Ruth's nationality is twice stressed; Boaz has been forewarned and should back away from the Moabite.

In the perfect world of the fussy, post-exilic sectarians, Ruth, a poor, foreign, distant relative who lives with her mother-in-law, is an inappropriate candidate for a wife for any self-respecting Jew. But, Boaz seems unfazed by these social and religious taboos; in fact, he appears to be quite smitten with the exotic Ruth and becomes her protector. He instructs Ruth to glean only in his field, under his watchful eye, so that she may avoid unwanted advances from randy reapers.

When Ruth expresses her gratitude, Boaz tells her that this is the least he can do for such a loyal and faithful daughter-in-law. News spreads quickly in small towns and Boaz has heard about the widow Ruth's selfless devotion to her mother-in-law (Ruth 2:11–12). A noble and caring man, Boaz admires the Moabite's generous nature. He invites her to eat at his table and even instructs his servants to give her extra grain (Ruth 2:14–16). After a long day of gleaning, Ruth returns to Naomi, laden with grain and news of the wealthy kinsman. Naomi is delighted with Ruth's news and she recognizes Boaz as a possible redeemer (*go'el*) who might rescue the widows from their present predicament. In the Bible, the term *go'el* usually refers to either a blood avenger for a relative who has been murdered (Josh. 7:24–25) or a male relation who acts as a protector to vulnerable relatives in danger of losing ancestral property (Lev. 25:25–55). It is likely that Naomi views Boaz in terms of the latter. (Later in the Bible, the *go'el* is a term used for the Lord and associated with God's saving actions [Isa. 41:14; 43:1; 52:3; Hosea 13:14].)

As Naomi listens to Ruth's adventures, she begins to hatch a plan. Naomi and Ruth are vulnerable; they need food, a place to live, and a safe and secure future. Ruth needs a rich husband—one who has no problems with Moabite girls and their mothers-in-law—and Boaz seems a perfect candidate.

Scene four (Ruth 3:1–18) begins with Naomi's well-conceived strategy for Ruth's seduction of Boaz. That Israelite Naomi is the architect of such a plan is hugely ironic considering the fact that it is the Moabites who are known for their sexual licentiousness. Perhaps Naomi picked up a trick or two during her ten-year stay in Moab.

Naomi instructs Ruth to bathe, anoint herself, and to put on her best dress. Once gussied up, Ruth is to go down to the threshing floor where Boaz and his men will be working and lurk in the shadows. After the men have finished their work and have their meal, Ruth is to observe where Boaz plans to bed down for the night. Once he is asleep, Ruth, the vixen, will join him on the threshing floor, uncovering "his feet," often in the Bible a euphemism for genitals. Naomi instructs Ruth to tell Boaz: "All that you tell me I will do" (Ruth 3:5).

The ever-obedient Ruth follows her mother-in-law's R-rated plan nearly to the letter. When the startled Boaz awakes to find Ruth lying down next to his uncovered "feet," he asks: "Who are you?" and she replies: "I am Ruth, your servant; spread your cloak over your servant, for you are next-of-kin" (Ruth 3:9). Notice that Ruth does not ask Boaz what *she* should do, a slight departure from Naomi's instructions; instead, she tells him to spread his cloak over her, a symbolic action signifying engagement.

The sexual innuendos in this story cannot be overlooked. In addition to the use of the euphemistic word "feet" (Ruth 3:4, 7, 8, 14) is the repeated use of the verbs "to lie down" (Ruth 3:4, 7, 8, 13, 14) and "to know" (Ruth 3:3, 14), both of which connote sexual intercourse. Still, the text does not explicitly state that Ruth and Boaz had sexual relations on the threshing floor. It seems likely that what we are dealing with here is a steamy love scene between two people who are mightily attracted to one another. Considering the author's intention to present Ruth, and presumably other foreign women like her, in a favorable light, it seems unlikely that the anonymous writer would tarnish her image by scripting a romp in the hay with her redeemer.

Whatever happened that night, the end result is that Ruth gets a husband and the two widows have their *go'el*; but there is a slight problem. Boaz informs Ruth that there is another, more closely related kinsman, whose claim must be honored before his own. Rather than spoil their little love nest, however,

Boaz reassures Ruth that all of this will be worked out in the morning and Ruth remains beside Boaz until the predawn hours. To avoid the walk of shame and possible damage to their reputations, Boaz sends Ruth home, with six measures of barley, before everyone else rises. Once again, she returns to Naomi with food and news, and the two wait for the results of the battle of the kinsmen.

Scene five (Ruth 4) opens with Boaz and the kinsman—whose name is rendered the equivalent of Joe Schmo or John Doe in the Hebrew—presenting their case to the city elders. Initially, Joe Schmo stakes his claim on Naomi's ancestral property, as is his right. When Boaz informs him that the property also comes with Ruth (and, ostensibly, Naomi), Joe Schmo reconsiders and withdraws his claim. Scholars debate the meaning of this rather confusing court case and most agree that it has something to do with the levirate law (Deut. 25:5–10). The levirate law states that a man's brother must marry his childless widow and that their firstborn son acquires the inheritance of the dead husband. Although there is some confusion regarding the extension of this law to other relatives, the text seems to indicate that there may be variations within the law of levirate and that the kinsman is required to produce an heir for Mahlon. If the levirate law is at work here, it is no wonder Mr. Schmo withdraws his claim.

With the messy issue of property resolved, we are ready for a happy ending. Boaz marries Ruth and, with another echo of the levirate law, proclaims their union as a continuation of the family of Mahlon (Ruth 4:10). The townspeople bless Ruth, invoking the names of the matriarchs Rachel and Leah (Gen. 29–30) and the wily Tamar (Gen. 38).

Boaz and Ruth continue the line toward David, producing a son, Obed, David's grandfather. Once Obed is born, Ruth disappears from the story as the author focuses on the restoration of Naomi and the prominence of the child in the Davidic line. The connection between the Moabite's son and David is highly significant and indeed, at least from the author's point of view, the high point of the story. Connecting Ruth to King David blurs the lines drawn by the post-exilic leadership that forbids intermarriage and asserts that nice girls like Ruth are acceptable after all.

Naomi, the bereaved, childless widow, who returns to her homeland in emptiness and despair, is thrice redeemed; first by Ruth, her loyal and faithful daughter-in-law, then through Boaz the *go-el*, and finally through the child Obed, the symbol of God's efficacious friendship and enduring love.

Ruth's Enduring Lessons

The story of Ruth begins with emptiness, barrenness, and displacement and ends with fullness, a child, and restoration of the land to Naomi's family. As such, Ruth has much to teach us about life's dual lessons of love and loss.

Ruth's much-admired loyalty and dedication to her mother-in-law is conveyed through her actions and in her moving profession of faith and devotion (Ruth 1:16–17). She remains with Naomi, forsaking her family, her country, and even her god. And she makes certain that Naomi is fed, cared for, and protected. Moreover, Ruth is obedient, following her mother-in-law's advice and directives, even though they might threaten Ruth's reputation.

Ruth mediates Naomi's bitterness and emptiness with food, shelter, friendship, and the blessing of a grandson. Yet, through it all, Naomi never expresses gratitude, nor does she praise Ruth for her fidelity and kindness. Which leads us to question why Ruth gives up so much to companion Naomi. *Why bother?* Ruth's devotion and loyalty is not based on reward or approval; her actions are grounded in the Hebrew concept of *hesed*, or loving kindness, and thus exemplify the nature of self-sacrificing love.

As we examine our own relationships with family, friends, and colleagues, Ruth's story urges us to seek new ways to express love and to demonstrate kindness, without the expectation of reward. But this is not always so easy; children are challenging, spouses and partners can be disagreeable, bitter mothers-in-law can be draining, and friends and colleagues are often fair-weathered and ephemeral. Moreover, when we help others, most of us want our good deeds to be recognized. In short, it is tough to be like Ruth. *Why bother?*

Ruth teaches us that self-sacrificing love is not motivated by ego or the need to have someone express gratitude. It comes from a different place within us that puts the needs of an individual or group before our own. When we do this, we connect with others on a deeper level, one that is free of attached strings and returned favors. Acts of self-sacrificing love bring about their own unique rewards, not only for the recipient of our kindness, but for us, too. Just ask any parent, anyone who volunteers in an animal shelter or works with the poor. Actions motivated by self-sacrificing love enable us to share our many gifts and talents with others and remind us of our many blessings. Such actions can also foster abiding friendships, temper loneliness, elicit reciprocal acts of kindness, and help us to remember that we are all children of God.

Ruth's story teaches us something about love, but it also teaches us something about loss. Naomi and Ruth return to Bethlehem in the throes of grief. Not only has Ruth lost her husband, but also her country, her god, and will likely never see her family in Moab again. Naomi loses her husband and *both* of her children, an unimaginable grief. In the world of biblical antiquity, where God is responsible for both "weal and woe" (Isa. 45:6–7), it is not surprising that Naomi directs her bitterness toward the Lord. Viewed in the context of profound grief, however, her bitterness is an understandable and appropriate response.

Perhaps Naomi's grief accounts for her lack of affirmation and gratitude for Ruth's many sacrifices. Anyone who has ever experienced the loss of a loved one can attest to the fact that we often say and do things out of character when we are bereaved and perhaps Ruth accepts Naomi's behavior as part of her overall grief response. In fact, Ruth's loyalty to Naomi is probably based on the loving friendship the two shared before the tidal wave of grief swept over them. Ruth remembers the old Naomi and accepts the grieving one.

The story does not record Ruth's reaction to the death of Mahlon nor does it detail the pain she must have felt leaving her homeland and family. Ruth becomes Naomi's caretaker at a time when she, herself, also needed a little *hesed*. Thus, her loving actions are even more meaningful when we consider the fact that Ruth, too, is in mourning.

As we examine this story in light of Naomi's and Ruth's grief, we learn that grief takes many forms. Some, like Naomi, may be more overt in their expressions of loss and may even feel bitter and angry. Others, like Ruth, may be more circumspect and less likely to express their grief to others. Of course, there are no rules for grief and each person grieves in his or her own way. But one thing is for certain: grief changes us. Naomi bears witness to this truth. Sometimes, profound loss can destroy individuals and even whole families. But more often than not, grief transforms and humbles us. It teaches us to be more compassionate, less judgmental, and certainly more grateful for those we love.

The alliance between Ruth and Naomi is an unlikely one. Few modern mothers-in-law and daughters-in-law can relate to the sort of relationship these two widows share. Yet, their shared experience of love and loss and their movement from despair, to hope, to final redemption, offers us hope as well.

Though most scholars view the book of Ruth as an important social commentary on the post-exilic prohibition against mixed marriages, Ruth's story is much more. Ruth moves beyond the narrow-minded, tribal leadership of the fifth century B.C.E. and addresses the unspeakable sorrows that sometimes come without warning into our lives, and the redeemers who step forward to help us navigate the painful sea of loss.

The Witch of Endor: Lawbreaker
Not a Ghost of a Chance

(1 Sam. 28)

Immediately Saul fell full length on the ground, filled with fear because of the words of Samuel; and there was no strength in him, for he had eaten nothing all day and all night. The woman came to Saul, and when she saw that he was terrified, she said to him, "Your servant has listened to you; I have taken my life in my hand, and have listened to what you have said to me. Now therefore, you also listen to your servant; let me set a morsel of bread before you. Eat, that you may have strength when you go on your way." He refused, and said, "I will not eat." But his servants, together with the woman, urged him; and he listened to their words. So he got up from the ground and sat on the bed. Now the woman had a fatted calf in the house. She quickly slaughtered it, and she took flour, kneaded it, and baked unleavened cakes. She put them before Saul and his servants, and they ate. Then they rose and went away that night (1 Sam. 28:20–25).

T HE STORY of the Witch of Endor—and her dramatic encounter with King Saul—is a little-known biblical tale about fear, hopelessness, and desperation; but it is also a story of mercy, compassion, and great courage. Many contemporary readers are surprised to find a story about a witch in the pages of the Bible. Modern images of witches in big black hats riding broomsticks, however, are a far cry from the type of witch found in 1 Samuel 28. The Witch of Endor can best be described as a medium, or one who has the power to contact the dead. She represents that segment of the population that retains belief in the pre-Yhwh, tribal superstitions, often in conjunction with the worship of The One.

To better understand the story of the Witch of Endor, let us take a look at Israel's first king, Saul, whose modest beginnings, ascension to the throne, and fall from the Lord's favor, often take a back seat to the more popular tales of Israel's charismatic and swashbuckling *second* king, David. For though his kingship often shrinks in the shadows of David's story (it is David's rise to power that predominates much of the books of Samuel), the Witch of Endor is uniquely connected to Saul.

The young Saul is described as a tall, handsome, unassuming, stone-kicking country boy (1 Sam. 9:2); when the reader first encounters Saul, he is wandering about in search of his father's lost donkeys (1 Sam. 9:6–7). Even as Saul is looking for the lost animals, the prophet Samuel suddenly receives a revelation from the Lord concerning the youth's destiny: Saul is to be the ruler of the people (1 Sam. 9:14–17). Approaching an initially reluctant Saul, Samuel eventually succeeds in anointing the farm boy as leader of the people. (Interestingly, in the course of these rites, Saul is never actually called "king" but rather "commander" [in Hebrew, *nagid*] of the people.)

Fulfilling his role as commander, the once-reticent new monarch has several successful initial exploits, including a stunning victory over one of Israel's archenemies, the Ammonites (1 Sam. 11). These early successes, however, are short-lived.

Perhaps it is his lack of maturity, poor counsel from those close to him, or the inevitable corruption that comes with power, but Saul, and his kingship, soon begin to unravel through a series of foolish, heretical, and politically inept episodes. Saul's downward spiral is one of the most tragic stories in the Bible.

Saul's undoing begins in 1 Samuel 13 when he takes credit for a military victory won by his son, Jonathan. Then, growing impatient before a battle with the Philistines, Saul fails to wait for Samuel, the priest and prophet, to arrive to offer the pre-battle sacrifice and instead offers the sacrifice himself, a cultic no-no. Samuel, who arrives just after Saul has performed a religious function normally reserved for Israel's priests, makes it clear that Saul's actions will not go unpunished: "Samuel said to Saul, 'You have done foolishly; you have not kept the commandment of the Lord your God . . . your kingdom will not continue'" (1 Sam. 13:13–14).

The prophet's words are fulfilled, as Saul slowly loses control—of his kingdom, his family, and ultimately, his very senses. He swears rash oaths (which, in the ancient world, are seen as binding) and begins to fight battles not so much for the glory of *God*, as for his own glory, which is something that always yields disastrous consequences in the Bible. For these and other sins, God sends a "tormenting spirit" to harass Saul (1 Sam. 16:14). And, in what modern psychologists might label schizophrenia or some other profound mental disorder, this "tormenting spirit" causes Saul to become severely depressed; plagued by strange voices and visions, he is consumed with paranoia.

The tormenting spirit symbolizes the fact that the Lord has abandoned Saul (1 Sam. 15:26; 16:14). Soon the people, including members of his own family, are fearful of his uncontrolled outbursts and bizarre behavior and they, too, begin to distance themselves from him. He stands alone, mired in his own insanity while the ambitious would-be king, David (a "man after the Lord's heart," 1 Sam. 13:14), grows in popularity. Eventually, the people (including Saul's own children) switch their alliances in favor of the politically savvy David, and the tormenting spirit's destruction of Saul is nearly complete.

Broken and hopeless, Saul becomes a shadow of the strapping country boy once favored by the Lord. And yet, even with his kingship in tatters, the dreaded Philistines are on the move, and Saul must somehow gather the strength to fight. Now that Samuel is dead (1 Sam. 28:3) and the people have aligned themselves with David, to whom can Saul turn for counsel? He turns to God, using traditional methods, including prayer, dream messages, prophecy, and even the *Urim* (sacred objects probably similar to dice, used as way to ascertain the Divine Will) but all fail him: "When Saul inquired of the Lord, the Lord did not answer him" (1 Sam. 28:6).

Consumed with fear and half-crazed, Saul reasons that if the Lord will not answer him, perhaps he can at least find a way to contact the deceased prophet, Samuel. Surely Samuel would know how to proceed with the Philistines. In order to contact Samuel's ghost, however, Saul must engage the services of a medium—the Witch of Endor.

Before we discuss the role of the Witch (sometimes called the *Necromancer* of Endor), we must note two important facts. First, the very act of consulting mediums is forbidden in Israel (Lev. 19:31; 20:6, 27); and second, it is Saul himself who drives out the necromancers and magicians from the land (1 Sam. 28:3), going so far as to issue the death penalty for anyone found guilty of engaging in sorcery (1 Sam. 28:9–10). The Lord alone has the power to preserve or punish. Mediums, magicians, and sorcerers threaten this strict monotheistic system with their smoke and mirror tricks; Saul, on religious grounds, bans them from leading the faithful astray. Indeed, in the stark summation of the author(s) of 1 Chronicles, Saul's interaction with the necromancer is one of the crimes that led to his death:

> Saul died because he was unfaithful to the Lord; he did
> not keep the word of the Lord and even consulted a
> medium for guidance, and did not inquire of the Lord.
> So the Lord put him to death and turned the kingdom
> over to David son of Jesse (1 Chron. 10:13–14).

It is ironic then, that Saul should violate his own decree
and seek the help of the Witch. But Saul is desperate—and desperate people do desperate things. So it is that the king disguises himself and travels (with two of his servants) by night
to Endor, a small village close to Mt. Tabor near Jezreel, to
consult the Witch (1 Sam. 28:8). Initially, she is suspicious and
fears a trap:

> The woman said to him, "Surely you know what Saul
> has done, how he has cut off the mediums and wizards
> from the land. Why then are you laying a snare for my
> life to bring about my death?" (1 Sam. 28:9).

But Saul reassures her with the promise of discretion and
the Witch seems convinced of her client's sincerity. Saul asks
her to conjure up the spirit of Samuel and as soon as she
catches sight of the ghost, she recognizes him as the king's
prophet. To her horror, she also realizes her patron is none
other than Saul: "Why have you deceived me? You are Saul!"
(1 Sam. 28:12). Once again, the King reassures her and asks
her to continue. Apparently unable to see the apparition himself, Saul asks the Witch, "What do you see?" (1 Sam. 28:13).
In a halloweenish scene that rivals any modern "Tales From
the Crypt," the Witch relates her vision to the king: "I see a
divine being coming up out of the ground . . . An old man is
coming up; he is wrapped in a robe" (1 Sam. 28:13–14).
Convinced that the ghost is Samuel, Saul bows down to
the ground and the Witch fades into the background. The
focus now is on the conversation between Saul and the spirit

of Samuel, who seems annoyed at the intrusion: "Why have you disturbed me by bringing me up?" (1 Sam. 28:15).

It is worth noting that Israel has no tradition of post-mortem existence as such. The general consensus is that the dead dwell for a time in a dark, cold, underworld called *Sheol* (sometimes mistranslated in English Bibles as hell) before simply disappearing. This story, then, is most intriguing. Some scholars believe it has its origins in Canaanite mythology, while others cite ancient rabbinic sources that held that the spirits of the dead hovered close by for a year before disappearing, which would make Samuel available for the Witch's summons.

In any case, the conversation between Saul and the ghost is a sobering one. Samuel informs the king that he and his sons will die the next day in battle (1 Sam. 28:19), a terrible prophecy that comes utterly to fruition (1 Sam. 31:6). When Saul hears this, he collapses on the ground, terrified and weak, "for he had eaten nothing all day and all night" (1 Sam. 28:20). (It is interesting to note that later, in 2 Samuel 12, King David will also lie on the floor, paralyzed with grief, as his infant son slowly dies—a punishment inflicted by the Lord for David's sin with Bathsheba.)

As Saul lay helpless on the floor, the Witch of Endor reenters the story and entreats the king to eat. Perhaps she has encountered this sort of reaction in her patrons before and realizes that there is little to be done, other than to offer the comfort of food. But the *way* in which she offers the sustenance is significant. For, sensing that the king is too distraught and would likely refuse, she does not simply offer to prepare a meal. Instead, she reasons with him, pointing out that as she has done him a great favor, he is now obliged to do what she asks:

> "Your servant has listened to you; I have taken my life in my hand, and have listened to what you have said to me. Now, therefore, you also listen to your servant; let me set

a morsel of bread before you. Eat, that you may have strength when you go on your way" (1 Sam. 28:21–22).

At first he refuses, but the Witch is persistent and Saul finally relents. She then slaughters a fatted calf and bakes unleavened cakes—certainly a more substantial meal than the "morsel of bread" she initially promised—and Saul and his servants consume the meal. The food will serve to sustain Saul physically as he faces the challenges that lie ahead. Once the meal is over, Saul and his servants leave the Witch and disappear into the silent night.

The Witch of Endor's Enduring Lessons

Every life is afflicted with suffering; this truth was as apparent to the biblical authors as it is to us today. Although we spend most of our lives trying to avoid pain, the truth is, in many ways, the measure of who we are—the mettle of our character and inner fortitude, and some would argue, the measure of our faith—can be revealed in the very moments of misery we try so hard to escape. Likewise, the manner in which we work to alleviate the suffering of others speaks to the heroine or hero in all of us. And, in a very real sense, the Witch of Endor is a heroic figure. An exemplar of courage, compassion, and fidelity, she becomes a powerful symbol for us today in several ways.

First, her conviction and devotion to her outlawed craft—which she continues to practice, even under the penalty of death—makes her a model of valor and resolve in the face of overwhelming opposition. For if rules and laws are just, then it is not simply because someone in power has decreed them. This truth is best illuminated both through actions of Saul—who first makes it a crime to practice sorcery and then violates his own edict by engaging the services of a sorceress—and the Witch who, even after she recognizes the disguised King, continues her work. And when she leaves the scene so that Saul can speak privately to the ghost, she has ample opportunity to flee, but she chooses to remain.

Moreover, it is clear from the story that the Witch is no charlatan; she really does bring forth Samuel from the grave. Her powers, then, at least according to the story, are real. Noteworthy, too, is the fact that the text makes no mention of an exchange of funds; absent is any of the typical Middle-Eastern price haggling. The Witch uses her gifts solely as a means to help others, rather than as a way to bilk money from desperate people—a trait often associated with modern psychics. All of this may account for the Witch's dedication to her vocation and her willingness to break the law.

Her actions remind us that it is the moral imperative of every person to remain steadfast in his or her beliefs, even when those beliefs do not square with the majority. Such tenacity of conviction is the hallmark of every religious reformer, every voice that speaks out against injustice, and every heroine.

The second enduring lesson has nothing to do with the Witch's psychic abilities—or even her courage to engage in those so-called forbidden practices—but rather her actions following the séance. Indeed, it is her kindness and compassion toward a terrified and badly shaken Saul that makes her one of the most appealing women in the Bible. Unlike the cranky spirit of Samuel, who delivers his stark, emotionless prediction of death and destruction, the Witch of Endor offers hospitality and real kindness. Both serve to somewhat ameliorate Samuel's harsh prediction.

The Witch is present with Saul during a moment of extreme duress and emotional turmoil. And, while her response in many ways typifies the role of women in the ancient world, by preparing meals and caring for others, it also transcends them. For the Witch of Endor ignores the social barriers of her day—specifically the gender roles and established protocols for interaction with the king—in order to help a fellow human in need. As Saul lies helpless on the floor, weak from hunger, and consumed with grief over the knowledge that he and his sons will die in battle the next day, the Witch—unlike the king's subjects, family, friends, and, even the Lord—does not abandon him. Instead, she gives him a hand up: "The woman urged him. . . and he listened. . . so he got up from the ground and sat on the bed" (1 Sam. 28:24).

Reaching out to others in the throes of grief or in the depths of despair is not easy. Our inclination is to look the other way, or to allow others who might be closer to the afflicted person to offer him or her solace. The Witch of Endor's unselfish compassion and loving hospitality enjoin us to be mindful of others, particularly those who are bereaved or otherwise emotionally distraught. Thus, this rather obscure biblical heroine teaches us that compassion comes in many forms and it is often the person we least expect who may come to our rescue during a crisis.

6

Jezebel: Liar and Lawbreaker
The Menace Beneath the Mascara

(1 Kings 16:31; 18:4, 13, 19; 19:1–2; 21:5, 7, 11, 14, 15, 23, 25; 2 Kings 9:7, 10, 22, 30, 36, 37)

His wife Jezebel came to him and said, "Why are you so depressed that you will not eat?" He said to her, "Because I spoke to Naboth the Jezreelite and said to him, 'Give me your vineyard for money; or else, if you prefer, I will give you another vineyard for it;' but he answered, 'I will not give you my vineyard.' His wife Jezebel said to him, "Do you now govern Israel? Get up, eat some food, and be cheerful; I will give you the vineyard of Naboth the Jezreelite."

So she wrote letters in Ahab's name and sealed them with his seal; she sent the letters to the elders and the nobles who lived with Naboth in his city. She wrote in the letters, "Proclaim a fast, and seat Naboth at the head of the assembly; seat two scoundrels opposite him, and have them bring a charge against him, saying, 'You have cursed God and the king.' Then take him out, and stone him to death." The men of his city, the elders and the nobles who lived in his city, did as Jezebel had sent word to them. Just as it was written in the letters that she had sent to them, they proclaimed a fast and seated Naboth at the head of the assembly. The two scoundrels came in and sat opposite him; and the scoundrels brought a charge against Naboth, in the presence of the people, saying, "Naboth cursed God and the king." So they took him outside the city, and stoned him to death. Then they sent to Jezebel, saying, "Naboth has been stoned; he is dead."

As soon as Jezebel heard that Naboth had been stoned and was dead, Jezebel said to Ahab, "Go, take possession of the vineyard of Naboth the Jezreelite, which he refused to give you for money; for Naboth is not alive, but dead." As soon as Ahab heard that Naboth was dead, Ahab set out to go down to the vineyard of Naboth the Jezreelite, to take possession of it (1 Kings 21:5–16).

THE PAINTED woman, femme fatale, and seductress who leads men astray, Jezebel is perhaps the most reviled woman in the entire Bible. Counted among the thin ranks of female biblical villains, her very name has become synonymous with female manipulation of the worst kind and no modern woman would appreciate being labeled a "Jezebel." But how did she earn such a torrid reputation? And what does the Bible really say about her?

Before we begin to explore these questions, it is important to keep in mind that the stories about Jezebel—and, one could argue, all of the stories in the Bible—are written from a particular point of view. We know that the author or authors who penned the tales about Jezebel found her utterly despicable—a fact made clear, first and foremost, in the Hebrew corruption of her Phoenician name, usually translated to mean "garbage pile" or "dung heap." As we can safely assume that her parents did not choose to name their princess daughter "dung heap," this etymological sleight of hand, a common practice in the Bible, serves as a warning to the reader: Beware! Jezebel is Israel's worst nightmare.

With this initial insight in mind, we must read Jezebel's story critically, with one eyebrow raised. So, legend and hearsay aside, what do we know for sure about this intriguing character?

A wife of King Ahab (1 Kings 16:31)—one of the rottenest kings in the Bible—Jezebel is the daughter of Ethbaal, the king of Sidon (or Phoenicia, located in modern-day Lebanon). Her marriage was likely part of a political alliance, as most royal marriages were in those days. Hence, Jezebel is an imported bride, a foreigner, which usually means Trouble (with a capital T). In the Bible, foreign wives are forbidden, not so much because they are foreign, but because of what they bring to the marriage—namely, their foreign gods. This seems to have been the biblical writer's major objection against Ahab's Phoenician bride.

Not all foreign wives are objectionable, of course; wives like Ruth, the Moabite, who convert are less threatening. But imported wives who choose not to bow down to the God of Israel are dangerous. They introduce new ideas and new ways of thinking, often influencing their husbands—which seems to be the case with Ahab. Indeed, the Bible tells us that he not only worshipped idols (1 Kings 21:26) but even went so far as to build a temple in Samaria for Jezebel's favorite Phoenician deities, Baal and Asherah. Moreover, Ahab regularly allowed the 450 prophets of Baal and the 400 prophets of Asherah to dine at the royal table (1 Kings 16:32, 18:19).

All this commingling of religion may be acceptable to Ahab, but the prophet Elijah—who, like most biblical prophets, serves as part of the Lord's morality police—is incensed by Jezebel's infusion of the Phoenician cult into Israel. Worse, for reasons that are not totally clear, Jezebel has apparently launched a killing campaign against the prophets of the Lord (1 Kings 18:4, 13, 19; 2 Kings 3:2, 13; 9:7, 22). Deciding he must put an end to this, Elijah challenges Jezebel's 450 prophets of Baal and 400 prophets of Asherah to a showdown on Mount Carmel (1 Kings 18:16–46). In what amounts to a "my God is better than your God" contest, the challenge has one simple rule: The deity who is able to ignite the fires beneath the sacrificial bull Elijah placed on an altar will be declared the One True God.

Despite a spectacular performance that includes prayer, pleading, dancing, and the grisly practice of gashing themselves, the prophets of Baal are unable to rouse their god. Not even Elijah's mocking suppositions as to Baal's silence—perhaps he is asleep, away on a journey, or relieving himself—can nudge their god into casting even the smallest of sparks beneath the holocaust (1 Kings 18:26–28). Not so when Elijah takes the stage. Predictably, a single prayer from the prophet evokes a miraculous response from the Lord. Fire falls from the heavens, consumes the bull, and Elijah emerges as the victor.

No longer the victim, Elijah is now the aggressor and it is time to exact revenge. In what amounts to nothing short of a bloodbath, he turns the tables on Jezebel and slits the throats of *her* prophets (1 Kings 18:38–40).

When King Ahab tells his wife what Elijah has done, she is outraged and sends a courier to Elijah with the following message: "So may the gods do to me, and more also, if I do not make your life like the life of one of them by this time tomorrow" (1 Kings 19:2). Elijah is terrified and decides it is time to get out of Dodge and, under the protection of Yhwh, escapes into the wilderness.

Aside from the drama of the contest and its bloody outcome, this story provides us with some valuable information regarding Jezebel as we move forward. Most notable is the fact that this sort of rivalry—between a man and a woman, especially a foreign one—is unheard of in the Bible. Jezebel goes toe-to-toe with Elijah, unrestrained by her husband, which means she wields considerable power apart from her role as wife and queen (although the Bible never actually bestows on her the latter title). Her fearlessness in taking on Elijah and his powerful God—and her subsequent vendetta against him for murdering her beloved prophets (notice that it is *Jezebel*, not the king, who issues a death warrant for Elijah) is significant, not least in Elijah's reaction to her death threat. After boldly slitting the throats of the 850 prophets of Baal, Elijah literally runs for his life—when threatened by a woman! This Elijah-Jezebel conflict demonstrates to us that Jezebel is a woman who, among other things, is used to getting what she wants, and that she will run roughshod over Israelite law in the process.

This total disregard for the law of the land is appallingly clear in the story of Naboth's vineyard (1 Kings 21). The story surrounds Ahab's desire to plant a little vegetable garden in a plot of land next to the palace compound. Unfortunately, the land is owned by a man named Naboth, who refuses the king's offer of a better vineyard or cash in exchange for the property because the land has been in his family for generations (1 Kings

21:1–3). Ahab is angry and deeply disappointed at Naboth's decision not to sell. He returns to his palace and sulks in his bed, too upset and depressed to even eat (1 Kings 21:4).

Jezebel, annoyed to find the king pouting and refusing food, decides to take matters into her own hands. As part of her clever plot to obtain the ancestral land for Ahab, Jezebel sends letters in Ahab's name to the elders of Naboth's village in which she writes: "Proclaim a fast and set Naboth at the head of the people. Next, get two scoundrels to face him and accuse him of having cursed God and the King. Then take him out and stone him to death" (1 Kings 21:9–10). Because of Jezebel's letters, Naboth is falsely convicted of blasphemy and treason, executed, and his property confiscated by Ahab (1 Kings 21:15–16).

It is clear that Ahab—as both king and an Israelite—demonstrates a total lack of respect for Israel's ancestral property laws. These laws expressly forbid the selling of ancestral land to someone outside of one's family (Lev. 25:10, 13–17, 23–24, 34). Hence, Naboth is not only legally within his rights to refuse the king's offer, but he is bound by religious obligation not to sell his property. Ahab as king would be aware of Israel's laws but Jezebel is from Phoenicia, and Israelite laws and traditions may be of little importance to her. Further, she may lack a certain understanding of Israel's laws and, as a member of the royal family, she may feel that she is somehow above the law. We might even surmise that the tactics she uses to obtain the land may be wholly in keeping with the royal maneuvers of her homeland.

And, let us not forget that while clearly reprehensible, Jezebel's actions are not at all dissimilar to the actions of many of *Israel's* kings—including David himself (recall, for example, David's arranged murder of Uriah in an attempt to cover his sin with Bathsheba in 2 Samuel 11). Jezebel, then, is just like *any* despotic royal; yet her actions receive a harsher censure by the biblical editors because of her gender, her nationality, and her religious affiliation.

Jezebel and Ahab are under the mistaken impression that they have gotten away with their crimes. The prophet Elijah reappears as he so often does in the books of Kings, seemingly out of nowhere, and warns the pair that the watchful eye of the Lord has witnessed their evil deeds and that there is a price to pay. Unlike poor Naboth, who suffered unjustly because of Jezebel's trumped-up charges against him, Ahab and Jezebel will get exactly what they deserve. Elijah makes it clear that Ahab's dynasty will come to a brutal end and that the king and his villainous wife will both die (1 Kings 21:19–25). According to Elijah, the body of Jezebel—as her name implies—"shall be like dung on the field" (2 Kings 9:37). The author attempts a modicum of rehabilitation regarding Ahab's role in all of this with the assertion that Ahab's crimes were the result of having been "urged on by his wife Jezebel" (1 Kings 21:26). Ahab is, after all, king of Israel and therefore worthy of some respect.

While Ahab dies a somewhat honorable death in battle, Jezebel is not so lucky. Indeed, Elijah's message of doom is fulfilled in the anointing of Jehu, the terrifying assassin king, who systematically destroys Ahab's descendants (2 Kings 9:30–37), including Joram, the son of Ahab and Jezebel. Recovering from wounds sustained in battle when Jehu arrives, Joram nervously asks: "It is peace, Jehu?" to which Jehu replies: "What peace can there be, so long as the many whoredoms and sorceries of your mother Jezebel continue?" (2 Kings 9:22). Jehu's comments refer to Asherah and Baal, Jezebel's beloved deities.

Joram attempts to flee, but crippled by his war wounds, he is an easy target. Jehu draws his bow and shoots him in the back, the arrow piercing his heart. Then, in what appears to be a bit of biblical poetic justice—and in fulfillment of Elijah's prophecy (1 Kings 21:17–23)—Joram's corpse is callously tossed into Naboth's vineyard (2 Kings 9:25–26). Leaving the dead unburied in Israel is scandalous; that Joram is a member of the royal family is even more shocking. Further, the text is chillingly clear here. Joram's death is directly related to his mother's behavior—in what Jehu views as her "whorish" religious practices—and her unjust treatment of poor Naboth.

Continuing his bloody rebellion, Jehu sets off for Jezreel to pay a visit to Jezebel. It is unclear whether or not Jezebel has received the news of her son's death, but her actions would seem to indicate as much. With the death of her husband and now her son, she has little else to lose, and in one final, defiant gesture, Jezebel, her hair adorned and in full makeup (both beautifications, redolent of foreign cults and viewed with disdain in Israel, see, Jer. 4:30 and Ezek. 23:40) faces Jehu.

She leans out of her window and taunts him and he roars through the gate: "Is all well, Zimri, murderer of your master?" (2 Kings 10:31). Her greeting, as well understood by the faithful reader as by Jehu himself, is profoundly insulting, for "Zimri" is a well-known assassin. This only hastens the inevitable: Tossed out of the window by her eunuchs, she is trampled to death by horses, and apparently eaten by dogs (2 Kings 9:33–35) in fulfillment of Elijah's prophecy (1 Kings 21:19). Fair or no, it is a truly tragic end to one of the Bible's most infamous bad girls.

Jezebel's Enduring Lessons

In reading Jezebel's story, we can't help but wonder: just how bad was Jezebel, really? Given her reputation as one of the Bible's most detested villains, some might argue that the biblical writers judged her too harshly—that she was, after all, merely a Phoenician girl who was transported to Judah in a politically motivated marriage alliance brokered between her father and Ahab. Viewed in the context of her overall foreignness, her worship of Baal and Asherah, then, might be viewed favorably; after all, one has to admire a person who holds fast to her religion in a foreign land. Indeed, Jezebel's allegiance to her gods gives us pause to question the depth and fortitude of our own faith. Could we persevere in faith under similar circumstances?

But, at least insofar as Jezebel is concerned, is there more to the question than that? For, when she takes upon herself to systematically slaughter the Lord's prophets, she crosses that proverbial line in the sand. It is all well and good to worship one's gods *alongside* those of another, what we might term "religious tolerance" today, but when one imposes those beliefs on another through the use of violence, such actions are morally indefensible.

Of course, we might also argue that Elijah—who, recall, killed 850 prophets of Baal and Asherah—is every bit as guilty in this regard as Jezebel. In fact, Elijah's showdown on Mount Carmel is less about the prophet and the princess and more about the polluting influences of foreign cults. And, we know that when the Bible speaks of something over and over again, it is a problem. For example, Israel's vacillating devotion to Yhwh is apparent in the biblical author's repeated condemnation of foreign deities. The appeal of the storm-snorting god Baal (mentioned 89 times in the Hebrew Bible) and the seductive, come-hither lure of Asherah (mentioned some 40 times) proved to be a constant threat to the faithful. The inflexible, sober God of Israel needed a few sentries. So, if we think of Elijah as a gatekeeper of the faith, then we are inclined to side with him in the contest. The reality, however, is that Jezebel and Elijah are mirror images of one another with similar goals and tactics: both believe that their god is superior; both promote their god above all others; and both will use violence as a means of eliminating the competition.

As far as her looks—the "excessive" hair adornment and makeup so condemned by the biblical writers—well, these issues, too, are cultural. In modern times, we chalk such differences up to "diversity," and condemning a person because of her religious beliefs or cultural differences would be considered rank discrimination. Even so, we must ask ourselves: How often do we judge others based on appearance alone? And how open are we to challenge conformity?

Setting everything else aside, one would be hard-pressed to justify Jezebel's behavior with regard to Naboth, but then again, her actions are comparable to the kinds of tactics traditionally used by men of the period in political warfare. In fact, most of Israel's kings were notoriously corrupt. We can't help but wonder if her condemnation by the biblical writer or writers is based less on her tactics than on her gender, religion, and nationality, as is the case with many other female biblical figures. So often in the Bible (as in life!), the enemy is demonized; and we can assume that Jezebel is no exception. While this may not make her actions any less reprehensible, it *does* give us pause. Finally, whatever other conclusions we might draw from her story, Jezebel, the beautiful, powerful, Phoenician princess reminds us that evil comes in many forms, and often goes hand in hand with power itself.

Victims, Volunteers, and Vindicators

The Widow Tamar, Miriam, Bathsheba, Tamar, Sister of Absalom, the Shunammite Woman, Susanna

"Charm is deceitful,
and beauty is vain,
but a woman who fears
the Lord is to be praised"
(Prov. 31:30).

The Widow Tamar:
Victim and Vindicator
Baby, You Owe Me
(Gen. 39)

When Tamar was told, "Your father-in-law is going up to Timnah to shear his sheep," she put off her widow's garments, put on a veil, wrapped herself up, and sat down at the entrance to Enaim, which is on the road to Timnah. She saw that Shelah was grown up, yet she had not been given to him in marriage. When Judah saw her, he thought her to be a prostitute, for she had covered her face. He went over to her at the roadside, and said, "Come, let me come in to you," for he did not know that she was his daughter-in-law. She said, "What will you give me, that you may come in to me?" He answered, "I will send you a kid from the flock." And she said, "Only if you give me a pledge, until you send it." He said, "What pledge shall I give you?" She replied, "Your signet and your cord, and the staff that is in your hand." So he gave them to her, and went in to her, and she conceived by him. Then she got up and went away, and taking off her veil she put on the garments of her widowhood (Gen. 38:13–19).

TAMAR, THE twice-widowed, infamous faux prostitute is one of the Hebrew Bible's most cherished folk heroines. Like Rebekah, she is a trickster character who manipulates events to help bring about God's plan. Her steadfast persistence in getting what is rightfully hers, and her rather unconventional means of attaining it, make her story one of the most fascinating in the Bible.

Tamar's tale appears as an interlude in the story of Joseph (later of *Technicolor Dream Coat* fame), and is sandwiched between the scene in which Joseph's brothers sell him into slavery (Gen. 37:27–28) and his near-seduction by Potiphar's lusty wife (Gen. 39). If Genesis 38 were excised, Genesis 37 would flow quite naturally into Genesis 39. Most scholars assume that the placement of Tamar's story between Genesis 37 and 39 has something to do with its connection to Joseph's brother, Judah, the antagonist in the Tamar saga.

Genesis 38 begins with Judah, one of Jacob's twelve sons, leaving his family and settling just outside Bethlehem. He marries a local Canaanite woman and they are blessed with three sons, Er, Onan, and Shelah (Gen. 38: 2–5). The biblical author does not comment on the fact that Judah marries a Canaanite rather than a nice Israelite girl, but the blessings of three sons indicate God's tacit approval of the union, at least at the beginning.

In typical fast-forward biblical fashion, the boys grow up in only a few verses. When the eldest, Er, is ready for a wife, Judah takes it upon himself to procure one for him. It is unclear if Judah fishes from the same pond in which he snagged his own Canaanite bride, but many scholars assert that Tamar, too, is Canaanite. While the Bible does not expressly state Tamar's tribal origins, the two people mentioned in close connection to Judah—his wife and his friend, Hirah the Adullamite—are both Canaanites, which bolsters the claim that Tamar is also Canaanite.

Tamar's nationality aside, her marriage to Er is a disaster. He does something—the Bible does not tell us what—that greatly offends God and God kills him (Gen. 38:7). Under the law of levirate (Deut. 25:5–10), which decrees that a surviving brother must marry his dead brother's widow, Judah gives Tamar to Er's younger brother, Onan. If Tamar has a son with Onan, according to the levirate law, her firstborn son is recognized as *Er's* and assumes primacy over Onan when it comes to inheritance. Obviously, it is not in Onan's best financial interest to have a child with Tamar, so he practices *coitus interruptus*, an action that prompts the Lord to kill him, too: "But since Onan knew that the offspring would not be his, he spilled his semen on the ground whenever he went in to his brother's wife, so that he would not give offspring to his brother" (Gen. 38:9–10).

It is not Onan's sexual behavior that provokes the Lord; rather, it is his refusal to honor the law of levirate. This is an important distinction because for centuries, this passage has been used to condemn the practice of masturbation. The term "onanism," taken from Onan's name, is an eponymous term for masturbation. As recently as the nineteenth century, onanism was considered both a sin and a medical condition that affected the brain and nervous system. Elaborate medical devices were prescribed for particularly stubborn cases to aid the afflicted in keeping his hands off of himself. While all of this may seem preposterous to contemporary readers, it is no joke, for it points to the larger problem of biblical misinterpretation. Onan's story illustrates how such faulty understandings of Scripture not only confuse the author's intent, but also can be downright dangerous.

In any case, Onan's death means that Tamar is once again without a husband. She is nonetheless still entitled to have children from Judah's family and the levirate demands that Judah must give to her his only remaining son, Shelah. But Shelah is too young to marry, so Judah sends Tamar away to her father's house to wait until Shelah is old enough to wed (Gen. 38:11). At least this is the story he tells Tamar. The reader, however, knows the real story. Judah thinks Tamar is a toxic bride and fears losing another son (Gen. 38:11). It is clear that he has no intention of allowing Shelah anywhere near Bridezilla, not now, not ever. While the reader knows the truth behind Judah's actions, Tamar does not. This makes her a sad victim of Judah's fears. The reader also knows that it is *God* who kills Er and Onan for offending him and that Tamar has nothing to do with their deaths. Judah, of course, does not know this, which helps to explain his actions.

Tamar returns to her father's house, a twice-widowed woman with no children. In the world of biblical antiquity, where a woman's value is largely dependent upon her ability to produce children, this is a humiliating experience. But Tamar trusts that Judah will honor the law of levirate as he has done in the past. Engaged to Shelah, she is not free to marry anyone else, so she waits for her future husband to become a man.

Time passes, Judah's wife dies, Shelah grows up, and Tamar eventually realizes her father-in-law's betrayal. Her situation seems desperate, but things change quickly when she hears that Judah will be passing through town on the way to Timnah for a sheep shearing (Gen. 38:13). Tamar seizes the opportunity and swings into action to take what is rightfully hers. Judah owes her a child from his family—now *her* family—and since Shelah has been safely sequestered away from her grasp, the seed must come from Judah. But, it is not so easy to trick a father-in-law into sleeping with a toxic daughter-in-law, unless there is a plan.

Although the story seems to indicate Tamar's actions are spontaneous, her plan is so ingenious, we cannot help but wonder if she conceives it over time, sketching out the details as the slow dawning of Judah's betrayal crystallizes in her mind. As Judah approaches Enaim, the main road leading to the town of Timnah, Tamar is ready. Removing her widow's garb and covering her face with a veil, Tamar waits on the side of the road, the place of streetwalkers, beggars, and unescorted women with dubious reputations (Gen. 38:14). Her disguise reminds us of Rebekah's hoodwinking of Isaac and the Esau costume she pieced together for Jacob.

Some scholars question Tamar's intentions; that is, does she plan to dupe Judah into sex by pretending to be a prostitute? Of course she does! Although the story does not explicitly state that Tamar dresses as prostitute, she is later referred to both as *zonah* (the generic term for a prostitute, Gen. 38:15) and *qedesah* (a term used for Canaanite sacred prostitutes, attached to the temple, who also perform a variety of other nonsexual chores, Gen. 38:21–22). Prostitutes during this time generally do not cover their faces, but surely, some do. And, Tamar apparently acts the part for when Judah spies her on the side of the road, he "thought her to be a prostitute." (Gen. 38:15). He approaches the bogus hooker and the two talk business:

> He went over to her at the roadside and said, "Come let me come in to you." For he did not know she was his daughter-in-law. She said, "What will you give me, that you may come in to me?" He answered, "I will send you a kid from the flock." And she said, "Only if you give me a pledge, until you send it." He said, "What pledge shall I give you?" She replied, "Your signet and your cord, and the staff that is in your hand." So he gave them to her and went in to her (Gen. 38:16–18).

This little conversation is quite revealing in several ways. It is clear that Judah does not recognize the widow Tamar; of course, her face is covered and perhaps she disguises her voice, but he obviously has no idea that the woman behind the veil is his daughter-in-law. Some scholars speculate that this is the author's way of distancing Judah from those nasty incest regulations in Leviticus that forbid sex between fathers-in-laws and daughters-in-law (Lev. 18:15), but the truth is, Judah *must* be unaware of the "hooker's" identity or else the story simply falls apart.

Judah also seems clueless when it comes to negotiating a fee for service with the "prostitute." To leave his signet and cord with her in pledge is the modern equivalent of giving her his driver's license! The signet is a ring or cylinder with distinctive markings or a signature that is used as a person's official stamp. It often hangs from a cord around the neck. It seems doubtful that Judah is stupid; rather, as a recently widowed man, he simply lacks experience with the protocols of the sex trade. Not so with Tamar, who has apparently done her homework. We can almost see her smirking under her veil as Judah hands over his identifying accoutrements.

The sex between the widow and widower is quick, but effective; Judah "went in to her, and she conceived by him" (Gen. 38:18). Thus, out of great losses—Er, Onan, and Judah's wife—comes life. After getting her due, Tamar returns to her father's house for a quick costume change back into her widow's dress, and once again, she waits. Judah attempts to compensate the "call girl" for her favor, and sends his friend Hirah, back to the entrance of Enaim where the brief encounter took place (Gen. 38:21). Hirah hopes to exchange the kid for Judah's personal effects, but no one seems to know anything about a prostitute in that area of town, so he returns to Judah, unsuccessful in his mission.

Three months later, Judah receives word from the locals that his daughter-in-law, Tamar, has been a naughty girl: "Tamar has played the whore . . . she is pregnant as a result of whoredom" (Gen. 38:24). In the honor-and-shame culture of the ancient Near East, Judah's entire family is shamed by Tamar's behavior. She must be punished in order to restore honor to Judah's family and he decrees that Tamar must be executed. A woman caught in adultery is usually stoned to death (Deut. 22:23–24), unless she happens to be the daughter of a priest, in which case, she may be burned to death (Lev. 21:9). It is unclear why he insists on the more severe form of execution for his daughter-in-law, but Judah demands that Tamar be burned.

In a scene right out of Hollywood, Tamar is "brought out" to be executed and we cannot help but wonder if Judah feels some sort of relief at the prospect of getting rid of Toxic Tamar once and for all. If he does, the relief is short-lived, for Tamar has the ultimate trump card up her sleeve. Face-to-face with the father-in-law who betrayed her, she produces the items Judah left in pledge during their brief sexual encounter on the side of the road. "It was the owner of these who made me pregnant. . .Take note, please, whose these are, the signet and the cord and the staff" (Gen. 38:25). And with that, the condemned Tamar is vindicated. We can almost hear cheers rising up from the ancient listeners who probably heard this story around the campfire.

After the years of waiting for what is rightfully hers, Tamar's vindication is all the sweeter when Judah is forced to admit: "She is more in the right than I, since I did not give her my son Shelah" (Gen. 38:26). Through his admission, Judah's character softens; perhaps he has a change of heart and realizes his own culpability. While the text does not state this explicitly, his admission marks a shift in the story, from death to life.

The story that begins with the death of two sons ends with the birth of two sons. Reminiscent of the twin birth of Jacob and Esau, Tamar gives birth to twin sons, Zerah and Perez. During Tamar's labor, Perez puts forth his tiny hand and before withdrawing it the midwife ties a crimson cord around his wrist, marking him as the firstborn. So, even though Zerah emerges first, he has been usurped by his brother's premature wave. Like Jacob, the supplanter, it is Perez who is favored because he is an ancestor of the great King David (Ruth 4:18–22). Moreover, the rivalry between Zerah and Perez (two clans from the tribe of Judah, Num. 26:19–22) reminds us of the rivalry between Jacob and Esau, not to mention the sibling rivalry between Joseph and the rest of his brothers, including Judah (Gen. 37). It is this latter rivalry that connects this otherwise independent tale to the larger narrative about Joseph.

Tamar survives the loss of two husbands, the humiliation of barrenness, the betrayal of her father-in-law, and near execution, only to emerge victorious in getting what is rightfully hers. Praised and admired for her courage, trickery, and skillful manipulation of events, she works within the restrictions of the patriarchal system responsible for her predicament to bring about justice, thus earning the reputation as one of the Bible's greatest folk heroines.

Tamar's Enduring Lessons

Why would a woman dress up like a prostitute and trick her father-in-law into having sex with her on the side of the road? And, what are we supposed to learn from this story of deception and manipulation? Indeed, reading Tamar's story without understanding its many nuances—such as the levirate law of inheritance—is confusing. This is precisely why her story is often overlooked among the great narratives in the book of Genesis, usually excised in the reading of the greater narrative about Joseph, and why we rarely hear mention of her name in sermons or in the classroom. Tamar appealed to ancient listeners because of her much-admired trickery and courage, but her struggles also speak to contemporary readers. Her story has much to teach us about the lies we tell ourselves, the painful realities of betrayal, and the risks involved in change. Her story also inspires us to question the status quo, to challenge authority, and to patiently work toward justice.

Tamar's story begins with almost banal predictability. She is a young bride, starting a new life with a new family in a new place. Like most newlyweds, her life is filled with hope for future happiness with her new husband and, eventually, children. But the familiar story of wedded bliss and babies suddenly goes terribly wrong.

Without warning, her new husband dies and before she is even able to mourn his death, she is thrust into a new marriage to a man who does not want her. Before long, he too dies unexpectedly and Tamar is once again displaced. The common thread in her disjointed young life is her father-in-law, Judah, who arranges both marriages and then ships her off to her father's house to wait for a third marriage that will never materialize.

In a life dominated by men, Tamar is powerless, voiceless, and marginalized. She is the ultimate victim. Thousands of years separate Tamar's plight from the realities of modern living and although contemporary women may feel they have little in common with Tamar, the truth is, women in many parts of the world are every bit as powerless, voiceless, and marginalized. We are not just talking about particularly oppressive societies in far off corners of the world, but right here in the backyards of Western culture. Despite the common belief that we have come a long way, baby, sadly the opposite is true for many women today.

The subjugation of women often begins innocently enough, in childhood, with a common female mythology that has occupied the imaginations of countless little girls, in one form or another, throughout the ages. This mythology usually involves a white knight on a horse, translated: marriage, 2.5 children, and living happily-ever-after in a lovely house with a white picket fence. Today, the post-feminism backlash culture has produced a new crop of women who fully expect to be swept off their feet and taken care of by a Prince Charming in a variety of guises. But this mythology is the stuff of fairy tales.

While the longing to have a loving mate, a home, and children is a tangible and fundamental desire for a large portion of the population, for some women, like Tamar, life just does not turn out that way. Many women, by choice or circumstance, will not marry or have children. A greater number will wed, only to find that Prince Charming is not so charming after all. Some couples will not have children due to infertility, age, or by choice. And, for many women, the dream of a husband and family turns out to be a nightmare when they find they have partnered with an abusive mate.

Like Tamar, many women today embrace this mythology. As little girls, they tuck their dollies into bed, bake brownies in their pink toy ovens, and primp and preen their way through adolescence and young adulthood in hopes of attracting a husband and becoming part of the status quo. We can learn from Tamar that for many women, the status quo is an illusion, but we can also learn that even though the mythology can hurt us, it does not have to destroy us.

Tamar's story is very much a "rising from the ashes" story, for while she, like most women in her day and age, adheres to the mythology, it brings her nothing but heartache and humiliation. At some point, however, she realizes that in order to have what she wants—indeed, what is rightfully hers—she must be proactive and take it. Simply waiting for circumstances to change, or worse, trusting in someone to make changes for her has made her a victim. Creating a strategy and formulating a plan, however, empowers her to take charge of her life and her destiny. Perhaps this is Tamar's most enduring lesson.

Tamar's story teaches us to take charge of our lives, but she also teaches us that there are risks involved. Had Judah discovered her hoax, or had he decided to suppress the evidence of his paternity, Tamar's actions could have literally gone up in smoke. She must have thought about the possibility that her plan might backfire. But, in the end, with great courage and resolve, she takes the risk because the possible rewards are far greater than living a life on *Judah's* terms.

While we can question her tactics, we cannot help but appreciate her pluck and moxie. We must be ever-mindful, too, that Tamar's actions help to bring about God's plan through the continuation of the family of Judah and eventually King David, for these are important details the ancient writer sought to impart. Finally, Tamar the folk heroine, reminds us that certain circumstances require us to move from the sidelines, step up to the plate of our own lives—and swing.

Miriam: Volunteer
Big Sister Is Watching

(Exod. 2:4–8; 15:20–21; Num. 12; 20:1; Deut. 24:9;
1 Chron. 6:3; Mic. 6:4)

Now a man from the house of Levi went and married a Levite woman. The woman conceived and bore a son; and when she saw that he was a fine baby, she hid him for three months. When she could hide him no longer she got a papyrus basket for him, and plastered it with bitumen and pitch; she put the child in it and placed it among the reeds on the bank of the river. His sister stood at a distance, to see what would happen to him.

The daughter of Pharaoh came down to bathe at the river, while her attendants walked beside the river. She saw the basket among the reeds and sent her maid to bring it. When she opened it, she saw the child. He was crying, and she took pity on him. "This must be one of the Hebrews' children," she said. Then his sister said to Pharaoh's daughter, "Shall I go and get you a nurse from the Hebrew women to nurse the child for you?" Pharaoh's daughter said to her, "Yes." So the girl went and called the child's mother. Pharaoh's daughter said to her, "Take this child and nurse it for me, and I will give you your wages." So the woman took the child and nursed it. When the child grew up, she brought him to Pharaoh's daughter, and she took him as her son. She named him Moses, "because," she said, "I drew him out of the water" (Exod. 2:1–10).

PROMINENTLY featured in Israel's epic tale of liberation, Miriam is one of the most recognized women in the Bible. The eldest child of Amram and Jochebed (Num. 26:59; 1 Chron. 6:3), Miriam, along with her younger brothers, Aaron and Moses, escapes the shackles of Egyptian slavery and sets up new digs in the wilderness of Sinai. Though she assumes many roles, including protector, prophetess, and powerful leader, Miriam's most memorable role is that of sister. In fact, whenever Miriam is mentioned, she is always featured in the company of one or both of her brothers.

Miriam is a unique type of biblical female; she does not marry nor does she have any children. It is generally assumed that all men and women will eventually marry and women who choose to be single are virtually unheard of during biblical times. A woman who is not attached to a man is viewed with suspicion, the subject of mistrust and idle gossip. But this is not the case with Miriam and it appears that, at least for the author, Miriam's attachment to her brothers seems sufficient.

Miriam is featured in three separate scenes that frame the central epochs of Israel's emancipation narrative. In scene one, she appears as a child during Israel's Egyptian captivity. In scene two, Miriam leads the Israelite women in song following their escape from Pharaoh's army during the exodus event. In the third scene, she is the upstart sister who questions Moses' prophetic authority during Israel's sojourn in the wilderness.

Scene one opens with the people of Israel enslaved under the ruthless and paranoid Egyptian Pharaoh who fears the slaves will eventually rebel against him. His reasoning is that, since it is men who make war, the best way to prevent an uprising is to eliminate the male slave population. Apparently, Pharaoh has forgotten that his building campaigns benefit from male slave labor, but no matter. Pharaoh embarks on an extermination program, ordering the midwives Shiphrah and Puah to kill all male infants born to the Hebrew women (Exod. 1:16).

Demonstrating great courage and chutzpah, Shiphrah and Puah completely ignore Pharaoh's decree and continue to safely deliver both male and female Hebrew babies. Observing no measurable decrease in the infant slave population, Pharaoh demands an explanation. The midwives, apparently fabricating a lie on the spot, tell him "the Hebrew women are not like the Egyptian women; for they are vigorous and give birth before the midwife comes to them" (Exod. 1:19). Foolish Pharaoh accepts the midwives' outrageous story and now orders his people to throw all Hebrew male babies into the Nile (Exod. 1:22).

Saved by the midwives' refusal to follow Pharaoh's edict, Moses, the future liberator, is allowed to live; but his mother must hide him from the Egyptian officials (Exod. 2:2). After three months, she is no longer able to conceal her son, and for unknown reasons, she places him in a basket and sets him afloat down the Nile. It is here where we first encounter Miriam in one of the most touching scenes in the Bible.

Though the text does not yet name her, she is the big sister who stands among the bulrushes, keeping watch over her baby brother as he floats in his basket down the river (Exod. 2:4). This initial glimpse of Miriam is a prelude to the role she will play in the exodus and wilderness sagas. For while Miriam is an important figure in the chronicle of Israel's escape from bondage, her story is often eclipsed by her more popular brothers Aaron and Moses.

Miriam, at the ripe old age of seven, braves the shores of the Nile, the place of crocodiles, insects, and other creepy things, to follow the basket at a distance. In what appears to be a huge irony, the daughter of Pharaoh, who happens to be bathing in the shallows, spots the basket and sends her maid to draw it from the river (Exod. 2:5). Moses' name in Hebrew is linked to the verb "to draw out" for, not only is he drawn from the Nile, but he will draw his people out from the misery of slavery.

When the princess opens the basket, she finds the infant Moses crying and recognizes him as one of the Hebrew slave children her father sought to annihilate. The text informs us that Pharaoh's daughter, who is decidedly unlike her father, is moved with pity (Exod. 2:6). Miriam, concealed by the reeds, has been watching all the fuss. She observes that even though Pharaoh's daughter is aware that Moses is a Hebrew, and therefore subject to her father's decree, she does not turn the child over to the authorities, nor does she return him to the river, as we might expect. Instead, she feels sorry for the infant, but does not seem to know what to do next.

But Miriam knows what to do. In order for Moses to survive, Pharaoh's daughter must decide to keep him. There is much at stake and Miriam must act quickly while the princess's heart is still tender with pity. She does not express fear or trepidation in approaching the Pharaoh's daughter, and she speaks directly to her, bypassing the imperial attendants and ignoring the social conventions of the day that govern royal/subject discourse (Exod. 2:7). As if to sway the princess in favor of keeping the child, Miriam addresses a practical need and volunteers to help: "Shall I go and get you a nurse from the Hebrew women to nurse the child for you?" (Exod. 2:7). The child must be nursed and Miriam has someone in mind. Pharaoh's daughter is likely grateful for the offer and sends Miriam off on her quest.

In yet another twist, Miriam quickly produces none other than Moses' own mother, Jochebed, as a candidate for the job. And Pharaoh's daughter actually *pays* Moses' mother to nurse him! Once he is weaned, Moses is returned to the princess and he is raised under the nose of the Pharaoh, the very man who sought to destroy him (Exod. 2:8–10).

With its many ironic twists and turns, this entire scene seems like a carefully choreographed stage play. This leads us to question whether or not Moses' mother Jochebed and perhaps Miriam are the instigators of a larger plan to spare Moses' life. Based on her behavior, we might speculate that Pharaoh's daughter is a well-known person of compassion who openly disagrees with her father's appalling extermination plan. And perhaps Miriam takes notice of the time of day the princess is likely to be bathing in the river—and soon a plan to save Moses is hatched and flawlessly executed.

While the text does not explicitly state that Jochebed and possibly Miriam engineered the events that happened along the banks of the Nile that day, it does affirm that Moses' life is spared because of a celebrated circle of quick-thinking and courageous women: The midwives, who refuse to honor Pharaoh's command; Jochebed, who bravely hides her son and then sets him afloat down the river; Pharaoh's daughter, who adopts Moses as her own; and Miriam, the sister who watches over him during his precarious Nile journey and then brings him back home to be nursed by his own mother.

Miriam is again featured within a circle of women in scene two. With a little help from the Lord, Moses convinces the Pharaoh to let his people go (Exod. 12–31). As the Israelites joyfully leave their captors, they march toward the sea. But wait! Pharaoh suddenly changes his mind and sends his army after the former slaves, catching up with them and trapping them at the edge of the Red Sea. Moses appeals to the Lord for help and, in a scene best captured by Cecil B. DeMille in the film "The Ten Commandments," the sea parts and the Israelites safely cross to the other side. Pharaoh's army, however, is not so lucky. As they pursue the children of Israel, the sea closes in upon them and they all perish (Exod. 14:5–29).

In gratitude for their divine rescue, Moses leads the people in song (Exod. 15:1–18). After Moses' rather lengthy hymn, Miriam, here referred to for the first time as "prophet," picks up a tambourine and leads the women in song and dance (Exod. 15:20–21). In reviewing the dueling celebration songs, a disquieting question surfaces: Why does Moses get to sing such an impressively long song while Miriam gets only one verse? The growing consensus among scholars is that the song attributed to Moses (Exod. 15:1–18) may have originally belonged to Miriam, but that later editors assigned it to Moses. Regardless of whether or not this is the case, we *do* know that

Miriam's abbreviated song is considered to be one of the oldest poetic verses in the Hebrew Bible.

Her impressive designation as prophet indicates that Miriam occupies a leadership role within the community. That the women follow her in a song of praise to the Lord confirms this and lends a liturgical air to the event. It is interesting to note that while Miriam is called a prophet, there is no record of any of her prophecies. Commentators generally agree that her title comes from a later tradition that celebrates Miriam as a prophet.

Miriam's next appearance occurs in the book of Numbers, when she is featured, along with Aaron, "speaking out" against Moses' "Cushite wife" and challenging Moses' prophetic authority (Num. 12:1–2). Apparently, little brother has gone and married one of those forbidden foreign women the biblical authors tend to complain about (e.g., Deut. 7:1–5; 1 Kings 11:2). This curious passage leads many commentators to conclude two things: First, since Cush is the biblical name for modern-day Ethiopia, the wife in question is African. Second, the "Cushite wife" is not Zipporah, the first wife of Moses and mother of Gershom and Eliezer (Exod. 2:21–22; 4:20, 24–26; 18:2–6).

Others counter these assumptions, claiming that the foreign wife in question is indeed Moses' first and only wife, Zipporah. Zipporah was a Midianite whom Moses married in his youth, shortly after arriving in Midian following his murder of an Egyptian taskmaster for beating a Hebrew slave (Exod. 2:11–16). Scattered throughout the region, the Midianites lived mainly in the area east of the Jordan River and the Sinai Peninsula. The prophet Habakkuk links the Midianites with Cushan (Hab. 3:7), perhaps indicating that Cushan is a particular tribe of Midianites. It is entirely possible then that the Cushite (Cushan) woman in question is none other than Moses' Midianite bride, Zipporah.

Conversely, it is no secret that Moses and Zipporah had their share of marital problems, despite the fact that she once saved his life. In one of the most bizarre passages in the Hebrew Bible, Yhwh descends upon the unsuspecting Moses, intent on killing him. The event occurs during Moses' journey from to Midian to Egypt to liberate the Hebrew slaves (Exod. 4:25–26). There is no clear-cut explanation for the Lord's attack but Zipporah seems to understand what is required. Swinging into action, she takes a piece of flint, circumcises her son, touches the foreskin to Moses' feet (presumably, feet here is a euphemism for the genitals) and says, "Truly, you are a bridegroom of blood to me!" (Exod. 4:25).

Commentators have puzzled over this story and various theories have been put forth regarding its meaning. The most likely theory is that Zipporah performs a "proxy circumcision" by circumcising her infant son and then touching the foreskin to Moses. Whatever the meaning of the perplexing passage, the end result is that the Lord retreats and Zipporah joins the ever-widening circle of women who preserve Moses' life.

Moses seems to have a short memory, or perhaps he has other things on his mind. In any case, before the exodus event, he sends Zipporah and their sons away to live with her father, Jethro, a priest of Midian sometimes referred to as Reuel or Hobab (Exod. 18:2). Following the exodus, Jethro brings Zipporah and her sons to meet with Moses, and although Moses seems glad to see his father-in-law, the text does not report a happy reunion between husband and wife.

If Zipporah is not the Cushite woman mentioned in Numbers 12:1, then she is absent in the wilderness stories. Her death is not recorded and there is no mention of Moses' and Zipporah's divorce, so we are tempted to assume that they remained wed, but is entirely possible that they did not.

Of course, the identity question aside, we cannot help but wonder what is behind the siblings' complaint against the Cushite woman. Is it simply her nationality? Or did she do or say something that caused Miriam and Aaron, perhaps acting as a spokesperson for the community, to speak out? The text does not give us the slightest clue, but the most likely answer has to do with her foreignness and attachment to gods other than The One. This contention is supported by the many stories that exhort Israelite men to steer clear of foreign women and their dangerous deities. The complaint against Moses' wife likely has nothing to do with race but rather religion, as racism is (sadly) a more modern phenomenon.

Moses' choice of wife, however, is only half the problem. Miriam and Aaron also feel that their brother unjustly claims exclusive prophetic authority: "Has the Lord spoken only through Moses? Has he not spoken through us also?" (Num. 12:2). It would appear that, at least from his siblings' perspective, Moses is stealing all the glory. Miriam and Aaron are annoyed, and maybe a little envious of Moses' popularity, both within the community and with the Lord. In sum, the stress and uncertainty of wilderness life and the competition for leadership recognition seem to be behind Miriam's and Aaron's grousing.

Although Moses does not hear their complaints, the Lord does and quickly responds. Appearing in a pillar of cloud, Yhwh upbraids Aaron and Miriam and affirms his unique friendship with Moses. While other "lesser" prophets receive oracles the old fashioned way, in your run-of-the-mill "visions and dreams" (presumably, like Miriam and Aaron), the Lord speaks to Moses "face to face" (Num. 12:8).

After the divine tongue-lashing, the cloud departs and the Lord afflicts Miriam with a skin disease, most likely leprosy (Num. 12:10). That Miriam is punished and not Aaron is curious and leads us to reexamine both complaints against Moses. Scholar Rita Burns (See Resources) observes that the objections to Moses' Cushite wife and questions concerning Moses' prophetic authority are likely two separate stories, woven together in its present form. According to Burns, in the Hebrew text, the complaint against Moses' wife retains the feminine singular form of the verb, indicating that it was *Miriam* who raised the issue. If this is the case, perhaps this is the reason why she alone is punished.

As with most siblings, the quarreling is quickly put aside when one is in trouble. Miriam's brothers intercede on her behalf, but the Lord remains firm and demands Miriam be exiled from the community for seven days (Num. 12:11–5). Though the people are on the move, they do not strike camp and continue their sojourn but wait for Miriam to return to the fold. This last detail is significant, for it not only implies her leadership role within the community, but also indicates the community's affection for her (Num. 12:15).

Following her banishment from the community, Miriam disappears from the rest of the wilderness saga, until her death at Kadesh, briefly narrated in Numbers 20:1. Like her brothers, she dies before reaching the Promised Land, but the indelible image of the young girl on the banks of the Nile, who later sings a victory song, dress swirling, tambourine in hand, remains forever present in the minds and hearts of her people.

Miriam's Enduring Lessons

Though Miriam teaches us much about leadership, courage, and prophetic authority, her most enduring lessons strike us closer to home, for her story is first and foremost a story about family. In the larger context, the family is the children of Israel, a people whom God calls his own and the family to which Miriam belongs. The reciprocal love and devotion between Miriam and her wilderness family is obvious, particularly in the way they follow her in song after the sea crossing and the way in which they wait for her to return from her brief exile after she speaks out against Moses.

But if we move in closer and adjust our viewfinder, we bring into focus a trio of siblings, Miriam, Aaron, and Moses, a family so perfect in their imperfection, a family very much like our own. It is the special relationship between brothers and sister that draws us deeper into Miriam's story, filling us with the sense of the familiar, for we understand the joys and challenges brothers and sisters bring to our lives.

The sibling relationship is unlike any other, a mixture of affection and ambivalence, camaraderie and competition. And it is the only relationship that, in most cases, spans a lifetime. From cradle to grave—from childhood fears of monsters under the bed, to adolescent angst, to midlife crises—our brothers and sisters are our copilots, who travel beside us through the many phases of life. They are our solemn witnesses, the sacred scribes, who tell the story of our lives. Consequently, our siblings tend to know us better than anyone, including our parents. Perhaps this is why the sibling story is such a popular biblical motif; from Cain and Abel (Gen. 4:1–16), to Jacob and Esau (Gen. 25:22–34; 27; 32:9–21; 33:1–17), to Rachel and Leah (Gen. 29:9–35; 30:1–24), to Joseph and his brothers (Gen. 37; 42–50), what better way to teach a moral lesson? And so, it is no mistake that the author weaves a tale of three siblings who simultaneously help one another, resent each other, and pray for one another, into the greater narrative of liberation.

Viewed in the context of the sibling relationship, Miriam's questionable behavior in Numbers 12—her speaking out against Moses' wife and her questioning, along with Aaron, Moses' claims of sole prophetic power—is seen in a new light. Sisters and brothers often say and do things to each other that they would never say or do to anyone else. Because of the longevity and intimacy of the sibling bond, we often feel it is our prerogative to speak our minds, to point out character flaws, personal imperfections, and perceived behavioral aberrations in our siblings. While such conduct would signal the end of other relationships, brothers and sisters quibble and disagree, ignore or forgive, and then move on.

In other words, Miriam's and Aaron's tirade against Moses in Numbers 12 is considered less egregious because it is more about sibling rivalry. It is clear that the author agrees, for while Miriam is punished with a skin disease and a seven-day exile from her community, others who speak out against Moses and Aaron are not so lucky. In the terrifying tale found in Numbers 16, some two hundred members of the community challenge

Moses' and Aaron's leadership. When the Lord hears of it, the offenders and the apparent ringleaders, Korah, Abiram, and Dathan, along with their families, are either consumed by fire or swallowed alive when the earth opens beneath their feet.

The biblical authors often waded into the undertow of human relationships as a way to understand our connection to God. In many ways, the relationship between Miriam and her brothers reflects Israel's relationship with God. Miriam protects the infant Moses as he is set adrift on the Nile, just as the Lord protects the people during their dangerous wanderings in the wilderness. Miriam sees to it that the "abandoned" baby Moses receives sustenance and advocates Moses' own mother to serve as wet nurse. The people of Israel cry out to the Lord in the wilderness for food and the Lord sends an abundance of manna and quail. Miriam and Aaron speak out against Moses, challenging his exclusive prophetic authority, just as the people speak out against the Lord when the going gets tough in the wilderness, "Is the Lord among us or not?" (Exod. 17:7). And when Miriam is punished for her insolence and lack of faith, her brothers pray to the Lord on her behalf. Likewise, Moses pleads to the Lord on behalf of the people when they distrust the Lord and instead worship a golden calf (Exod. 32:11–14).

And so it is in families, large and small; sometimes we protect and defend, challenge and question, but always, we love. It is the special love between a sister and her brothers, between a prophetess and her people, and between a daughter of Israel and her elusive, unknowable God that is Miriam's most enduring legacy.

Bathsheba: Victim and Vindicator
No Man's Lamb

(2 Sam. 11; 12:9–24; 1 Kings 1:11–31; 2:14–25)

So Bathsheba went to the king in his room. The king was very old; Abishag the Shunammite was attending the king. Bathsheba bowed and did obeisance to the king, and the king said, "What do you wish?" She said to him, "My lord, you swore to your servant by the Lord your God, saying: Your son Solomon shall succeed me as king, and he shall sit on my throne. But now suddenly Adonijah has become king, though you, my lord the king, do not know it. He has sacrificed oxen, fatted cattle, and sheep in abundance, and has invited all the children of the king, the priest Abiathar, and Joab the commander of the army; but your servant Solomon he has not invited. But you, my lord the king—the eyes of all Israel are on you to tell them who shall sit on the throne of my lord the king after him. Otherwise it will come to pass, when my lord the king sleeps with his ancestors, that my son Solomon and I will be counted offenders" (1 Kings 1:15–21).

THE SUBJECT of countless sermons, moral injunctions, and artistic dep ions, the tale of Bathsheba and King David is one of the most well-known stories in the Bible. Bathing unaware on her rooftop, the beautiful (and very married) Bathsheba catches the roving eye of the lusty King David and is summoned to his palace to sate the king's sexual appetite. The two eventually marry and produce an heir, the great and wise King Solomon. While this is the popular version of the story, it is only just the beginning of one of the most captivating tales in Scripture.

The story of Bathsheba heralds a cycle of abuse-of-power tales starring Israel's largely incompetent and mendacious kings, most of whom receive harsh reviews from the biblical editors. A few are rare exceptions, like the religious reformer boy-king Josiah (2 Kings 22:1–23:30) and David who, despite his many flaws, remains steadfastly the Lord's undisputed favorite. The consistent condemnation of Israel's kings stems from the fact that most become power-hungry despots who love foreign women, worship foreign gods, and practice every form of social injustice imaginable. Through the mouths of Israel's prophets, however, God calls the kings to task. But, time and time again, the kings ignore the prophetic pleas to clean up their royal acts and instead continue to abuse the power entrusted to them by the people.

Bathsheba's story begins in the midst of a war against the Ammonites. The wife of a solider, a foreigner fighting for Israel, known as Uriah the Hittite, Bathsheba is left behind in Jerusalem hoping for her husband's safe return. By contrast, David, Israel's military leader, is not in the field with his men as a king in those days ought to be (2 Sam. 11:1), but is instead ensconced in his lush palace, taking naps, and prowling around on his roof, trolling for babes.

One evening, he notices a beautiful woman, Bathsheba, taking a bath on her roof. During biblical times, it is a fairly common practice to set various containers on the roof to catch the sparse winter rainwater. It seems likely Bathsheba collects the water in a small tub where it is heated by the sun for her bath. Decent men should look away when other men's wives are bathing, but David likes what he sees and asks his servants about the woman. He is told: "This is Bathsheba daughter of Eliam, the wife of Uriah the Hittite" (2 Sam. 11:3). This should be the end of the story, for Bathsheba belongs to another man. In fact, the author habitually refers to Bathsheba as "the wife of Uriah," (2 Sam. 11:3, 26; 12:9, 15) a not-so-subtle reminder that Mrs. Uriah is off-limits (even in the New Testament [Matt. 1:6], she is referred to not as "Bathsheba" but as "the wife of Uriah"). David, for that matter, has several wives and concubines of his own. If he wants sex, there are women who legally belong to him right there in the palace who would be more than happy to service the king. But, his liaison with Bathsheba is more than just sex; for David, the real aphrodisiac is power.

King David sends for Bathsheba and he takes her. Bathsheba's reaction to the royal summons is not recorded, but generally when the king calls, subjects, especially female subjects, obey. The portrait of David here is not very flattering: He is a man who sees, wants, sends, and takes; no matter that the wife of Uriah is not his for the taking. Once David has his royal way with her, Bathsheba returns to her home. Alone in her house, Bathsheba, the war bride, is soon faced with an uncomfortable truth: She is pregnant with another man's child. Bathsheba sends a message to David, informing him of the situation, and David quickly conceives a plan to cover his tracks. Summoning Uriah under the guise of receiving an update on the war, David spends some time with Uriah in a phony debriefing session before sending him home to spend the night with his wife: "Then David said to Uriah: 'Go down to your house, and wash your feet'" (2 Sam. 11:8). In the Bible, the term "wash your feet" is often a euphemism for sexual intercourse, a necessary prerequisite for David's cover-up plan. If Uriah has sex with his wife, everyone will naturally assume the child belongs to Uriah. But, unlike David, Uriah does the right thing. A solider on active duty is consecrated to the Lord and should remain with his men; accordingly, Uriah refuses to go home to eat, drink, and make merry with his wife, and chooses instead to stay within the palace compound with the rest of the king's servants (2 Sam. 11:9).

Throughout much of the story, the author skillfully contrasts Uriah, the one who does all the right things, with David, the one who does all the wrong things. With Plan A in shambles, David resorts to Plan B. Under the false assumption that a drunk soldier equals an amorous one, David plies Uriah with alcohol, but even drunk, Uriah does the right thing and does not return to his house (2 Sam. 11:13). When David learns that Uriah again did not go home to have sex with his wife, the story takes a decidedly more sinister turn.

David composes a letter to his field commander, Joab, instructing him to place Uriah on the front lines of battle where he is most likely to be killed. In a terrible irony, Uriah, the loyal soldier, carries David's death letter back to the front and gives it to Joab. Following David's orders, Joab, who is hardly a paragon of virtue himself, makes sure that Uriah is killed in battle and sends a "mission accomplished" message to David (2 Sam. 11:16–21).

With Uriah out of the way, David brings Bathsheba into his home, marries her, and she gives birth to their son. It would seem that David got away with his crime, but the Divine Eye has been watching David's elaborate cover-up scheme and the chapter ends on an ominous note: "But the thing that David had done displeased the Lord" (2 Sam. 11:27). As always in the Hebrew Bible, when humans displease the Lord, there is a price to be paid.

Speaking on behalf of the Lord, David's crime is brought to light by the prophet Nathan. In the Bible, the prophetic movement is closely tied to the monarchy and each king has a prophet who is, more or less, associated with his kingship. For example, King Saul and the prophet Samuel; King Ahab and the prophet Elijah; and King Hezekiah and the prophet Isaiah. Nathan, the prophet attached to David's kingship, confronts him with a parable about a rich man (David), a poor man (Uriah), and the poor man's beloved ewe lamb (Bathsheba). In the parable, the little lamb is "like a daughter" to the poor man, a clear play on Bathsheba's name (which means "*daughter* of the oath").

The rich man, despite the fact that he has many sheep in his herd (an obvious reference to David's collection of wives and concubines), takes the only lamb of the poor man and slaughters it for a feast with his guests (2 Sam. 12:2–4). David is outraged at the parable and proclaims that the rich man should be put to death for such an outrageous breach of social justice (2 Sam. 12:5). Like so many people who fail to recognize their own crimes, David must have Nathan interpret the meaning of the parable, proclaiming David as the rich man and the villain in the parable.

Admirably, David repents and the Lord preserves his life. But David's sons, four in all, including the baby born to Bathsheba, will pay for the sins of their father. The first son to pay is Bathsheba's baby: "The Lord struck the child that Uriah's wife bore to David, and it became very ill" (2 Sam. 12:15). While the idea that God causes innocent babies to suffer and die for the sins of their parents is repellent to contemporary readers, it nonetheless reflects the view of justice held by the author and most believers during biblical antiquity. In order to fully understand the rest of the story, we must keep this uncomfortable reality in mind.

When the baby falls ill, David keeps a fast and prays, hoping to sway divine judgment in his favor, but tragically the child dies (2 Sam. 12:18). David's reaction to both the child's seven-day illness and death are recorded in some detail. Strangely absent in the narrative, however, is Bathsheba's reaction. David fasts, wears sackcloth, sleeps on the floor, and pleads with the Lord on the child's behalf. After the baby's death, David changes his clothes, prays, and has a meal (2 Sam. 12:15–23). But David grieves from a distance. As in the war with the Ammonites, David remains detached from the thick of things; but Bathsheba, like her husband Uriah, enters into the fray.

We can imagine that Bathsheba continues to nurse her sick son as he fights for his life, that she holds him, and comforts him as he dies. Coming so soon after the loss of her husband, the baby's death is probably more than she can bear. Yet the text remains focused on the perpetrator of the crime, the instigator of all this misery, David. Bathsheba, however, remains a mute victim, presumably grieving in the shadows. David "consoles" her and she conceives and gives birth to another son, whom David names Solomon (2 Sam. 12:24). The name Solomon is variously translated to mean *peaceable* or *replacement*. Since biblical names often reflect an individual's role or actions in life, the latter translation seems more accurate, for Solomon is the one who replaces.

He replaces the baby brother who dies; he replaces his older brother, Adonijah, next in line to the throne; he replaces his father, David, as king; and in the famous story of two harlots claiming the same child, the first story attesting to his gift of wisdom, Solomon replaces the deceased child with a live one, restoring him to his rightful mother (1 Kings 3:16–28). These connections aside, the notion that a dead child—or any other human being—is replaceable is offensive to modern readers. Perhaps the Lord feels similarly, for he sends Nathan to rename the baby, Jedidiah (beloved of God). The child, however, is forever known as Solomon, the great and wise king, master temple builder, and a chip off the old Davidic block who cannot keep his hands off of forbidden women.

If we examine the story of Bathsheba thus far, we see her as a silent victim, caught up in David's megalomaniacal abuse of power. But her story does not end here. If we fast-forward to the next book in the Bible, 1 Kings, Bathsheba reappears, not as David's mute victim, but as a respected, powerful queen, who is not afraid to stand up to her husband and who now has plenty to say.

David, old and dying, shivers in his bed under a mountain of blankets, unable to keep his frail body warm. A beautiful woman, Abishag, is summoned to lie beside the king, to warm him with her body, but the author notes: "the king did not know her sexually" (1 Kings 1:4). This is the Bible's way of telling us that David is weak and feeble, for man's power is closely linked to his virility. Moses, by contrast, dies at the ripe old age of 120, but he dies in "full vigor" (Deut. 34:7).

David, now a weak old king, is vulnerable to a new crop of politically motivated royals, jockeying for position in the soon-to-be post-Davidic monarchy. Adonijah, David's son with wife Haggith, is next in line for the throne. Adonijah seems to have not only inherited David's good looks, but also his father's lack of impulse control. He throws a party for himself and prematurely proclaims his kingship *before* David's death (1 Kings 5–9). Adonijah, however, leaves two important individuals off of his party list: his brother Solomon and the prophet Nathan, neither of whom appreciates being snubbed.

Nathan goes to Bathsheba and tells her that Adonijah has crowned himself king without David's knowledge or consent and the prophet asks her to speak to David about the situation. It is here that we begin to see a transformed Bathsheba. Apparently, at some point in the past, Bathsheba negotiated a deal with David that secured Solomon's succession to the throne upon the king's death, even though technically, Adonijah is next in line. Nathan is aware of the deal and it appears that he and Bathsheba have forged a cozy little friendship. Nathan even helps Bathsheba script the meeting with David, so that she can remind the king of his promise regarding Solomon. Nathan will show up at the meeting in support of Bathsheba, and hopefully, the two will convince David to honor his promise. No longer David's victim, Bathsheba boldly appears before the king on behalf of her son. After an impressive, impassioned speech, David affirms his promise and promptly has Solomon anointed king (1 Kings 29–40).

Solomon's impromptu coronation puts a bit of a damper on Adonijah's party. When Adonijah and his cronies realize that Solomon kingship is secure, they literally run for the hills. Adonijah rightly fears for his life for kings in those days are prone to eliminate the competition. Though Solomon has ample reason to retaliate against his brother, he is remarkably restrained and spares Adonijah's life. That is, until Adonijah makes a foolish request. He asks Bathsheba to speak to Solomon on his behalf: "Please, ask King Solomon—he will not refuse you—to give me Abishag the Shunammite as my wife" (1 Kings 2:17). Bathsheba agrees to relay Adonijah's request to marry David's beautiful nurse and appears before the king. Solomon rises when she enters the room, bows down to his mother, and has a throne brought in for her so that mother and son may sit side-by-side (1 Kings 2:19).

We must pause for a moment and relish this scene, for in it, Bathsheba is presented as a power player in her own right. Not only does Adonijah respect her stature within the royal family, but also her son, the king, treats her as a co-regent. She has come a long way from her humble beginnings as a soldier's wife and David's pawn. She is a formidable, resourceful woman who engineers her son's political career thus gaining some political power of her own.

When Bathsheba relays Adonijah's request, Solomon smells a rat. Adonijah's desire for Abishag is nothing more than a political move. As David's nurse, Abishag has a wealth of insider information. For example, Abishag is present during David's personal conversations with Bathsheba and Nathan concerning Solomon's ascension to the throne (1 Kings 1:15–37; 2:1–10); thus Adonijah might find her useful should he challenge Solomon's kingship. Moreover, if Adonijah thinks he can take David's nurse, he might also try to take David's (now Solomon's) kingdom.

In a brutal blood-fest, Solomon orders the assassination of not only Adonijah, but also all of his brother's former supporters (1 Kings 2:24–46). Viewed in the context of a threat to the throne, Solomon's violent reaction is typical but what about Bathsheba's role in all of this? Does she agree to relay Adonijah's request to marry Abishag just to be nice, or does she have another agenda?

It seems likely that Bathsheba fully anticipates Solomon's reaction and views the inevitable bloodletting as a means to secure, once and for all, her son's kingship. She will not allow Adonijah, or anyone else for that matter, to threaten her son's claim to the throne. In short, Adonijah grossly underestimates Bathsheba's political acumen and commitment to her Solomon and inadvertently provides her with the means of eliminating a possible coup d'état.

Bathsheba's legacy, therefore, is that of a transformed victim—a survivor—who learns how to navigate the male-dominated world of palace politics in order to promote her son and to protect his interests. As such, she remains an enduring example of resilience, determination, and maternal devotion.

Bathsheba's Enduring Lessons

For two millennia, Bathsheba's story, as found in 2 Samuel 11–12, has been interpreted as the Bible's emblematic story of abuse of power. The great prophet Samuel forewarned the people that if they persisted in their demands for a king, they would be sorry, for kings tax the people, engage in wars, enslave the weak, and get wrapped up in their own power (1 Sam. 8:11–17). If, as the saying goes, absolute power corrupts absolutely, then Israel's kings, including David, surely embody this adage.

While 2 Samuel 11–12 reveals the fulfillment of Samuel's prophecy insofar as David's actions are concerned, it is only the first part of *Bathsheba's* story. The complete story of Bathsheba, rarely read in the classroom or discussed from pulpit, also includes the first two chapters of 1 Kings and details her amazing metamorphosis from David's hapless victim to a wise and influential queen. And, it is this rather startling transformation that is perhaps her most enduring lesson.

The Bible often uses role reversals to teach powerful lessons: The weak prevail over the strong; the younger is favored over the older; and women often outsmart the men. Bathsheba's transformation includes a complete reversal of established roles. Indeed, at the end of her story, David is the weak and vulnerable one, while Bathsheba assumes David's role, brokering deals and eliminating threats to the throne. For instance, her indirect role in Adonijah's death reminds us of David's roundabout way of executing Uriah. Perhaps the years of watching David operate taught her a thing or two. Although her methods may seem questionable to modern audiences, the use of role reversal is the author's way of demonstrating Bathsheba's change from victim to victor. Her unlikely transformation is a powerful lesson in the resiliency of the human spirit.

Bathsheba's ability to rise above David's initial victimization, to endure the loss of Uriah and her infant son, and to work within the patriarchal framework of Israel's monarchy, inspires us as we work to free ourselves from the shackles of the unfairness and misfortune in our own lives. At one time or another, most of us will fall victim to someone in power, whether it be an abusive parent, mate, friend, or superior in the workplace. Bathsheba teaches us that just because we are victimized, we are not doomed to forever bear the burden of that identity. She reminds us that there is something deep within us that cries out against injustice. It is this instinctual sense of fairness that lies at the heart of resiliency. And our ability to bounce back from adversity is the first step to regaining personal power, the antidote to victimization.

Personal power also allows us to forgive those who may have wronged us, often the final step in reclaiming wholeness. Forgiveness is not simply a gracious act we bestow upon the perpetrator, though it can certainly be that, nor does it necessarily include reconciliation. When we forgive, we liberate ourselves from the strangleholds of hatred and resentment, both of which bind us to the very person who harmed us. Moreover, we do not need to actually experience justice or restoration in order to overcome victimization. Resolve, fortitude, prayer, and other interior acts of courage also help us to reclaim our power. Bathsheba's story invites us to seek these and other antidotes.

Bathsheba, like Naomi (Ruth 1:1–5), is a bereaved wife and mother. She lives in a world where the Lord punishes the innocent for the sins of the father. Although it was David whom God sought to specifically punish (2 Sam. 12:13–14), we cannot ignore the fact that because of David, Bathsheba loses both her husband and child. How does one recover from such heartache and misery? We could hardly blame her if she remained mired in her grief, or became bitter, like Naomi. But something happens to Bathsheba that changes her: Solomon. Like Rebekah, the focus of her life becomes her son, for Solomon is Bathsheba's antidote.

Children, then and now, have a way of saving us from ourselves. They offer us hope for the future and they teach us what it means to sacrifice in the name of love. No longer weak and vulnerable, Bathsheba works to secure her son's future by negotiating a deal with David that guarantees Solomon's ascension to the throne, despite the fact that three of David's other sons (Amnon, Absalom, and Adonijah) are older and therefore more likely candidates to succeed their father. Bathsheba also garners the support of the powerful prophet, Nathan, God's official spokesman on earth. Considering the fact that Nathan is one of the few people who has intimate knowledge of David's crime, we can imagine that he feels a certain amount of sympathy for the woman who has lost so much. In the larger picture, Nathan's support of Bathsheba indicates that perhaps God, too, is on her side.

Bathsheba teaches us that change is possible, that we are stronger than we think, and that some things are worth fighting for; but she also teaches us that these things come slowly and often at great personal costs. Finally, her ability to transcend her circumstances and to shed the skin of victimization inspires us to work toward justice, to affirm our own dignity, and to care for those we love.

10

Tamar, Sister of Absalom: Victim

One Sick Brother

(2 Sam. 13)

So Amnon lay down, and pretended to be ill; and when the king came to see him, Amnon said to the king, "Please let my sister Tamar come and make a couple of cakes in my sight, so that I may eat from her hand." Then David sent home to Tamar, saying, "Go to your brother Amnon's house, and prepare food for him." So Tamar went to her brother Amnon's house, where he was lying down. She took dough, kneaded it, made cakes in his sight, and baked the cakes. Then she took the pan and set them out before him, but he refused to eat. Amnon said, "Send out everyone from me." So everyone went out from him. Then Amnon said to Tamar, "Bring the food into the chamber, so that I may eat from your hand." So Tamar took the cakes she had made, and brought them into the chamber to Amnon her brother. But when she brought them near him to eat, he took hold of her, and said to her, "Come, lie with me, my sister." She answered him, "No, my brother, do not force me; for such a thing is not done in

Israel; do not do anything so vile! As for me, where could I carry my shame? And as for you, you would be as one of the scoundrels in Israel. Now therefore, I beg you, speak to the king; for he will not withhold me from you." But he would not listen to her; and being stronger than she was, he forced her and lay with her (2 Sam. 13:6–14).

THE STORY of Tamar, the beautiful, virgin daughter of King David who is raped by her own brother, Amnon, acts as a bookend to the story of David's sexual crime against Bathsheba (2 Sam. 11–12). Tamar's brutal rape begins the fulfillment of Nathan's prophecy, a stark prediction that the house of David (meaning the *family* of David) would be destroyed from within (2 Sam. 12:10). As the house of David collapses like a house of cards, we must remember that the ensuing pain, suffering, death, and grief—including what happens to Tamar—are all part of the Lord's punishment for *David's* crime.

The Tamar of 2 Samuel 13 should not be confused with two other biblical women bearing the same name. Tamar, the subject of this chapter, is a daughter of King David, the half-sister of Amnon, and full sister of Absalom. Tamar's full-brother, Absalom, has a daughter, whom he also names Tamar (2 Sam. 14:27), perhaps as a way to honor his beloved sister. A third Tamar is the daughter-in-law of Judah, who tricks him into impregnating her (Gen. 38) and is unrelated to the two named Tamar in 2 Samuel.

The story of Tamar is a disturbing one, for ancient and modern audiences, as it is a brutal story of betrayal, rape, and a woman's life that is utterly destroyed through the actions of her own brother. Tamar's sad tale begins when her half-brother, Amnon, falls in love (read: lust) with her (2 Sam. 13:1). Amnon confides his forbidden desires to his friend and cousin, Jonadab, who is described as a "very crafty man" (2 Sam. 13:3), the Bible's way of telling us that he is a conniving liar. Jonadab conceives an elaborate ruse designed to lure Tamar into Amnon's bed. He instructs Amnon to pretend to be ill and to send for his father. When King David arrives, Amnon is to ask his father to send his sister, Tamar, to care for him by preparing and feeding him a medicinal meal (2 Sam. 13:5–6). Apparently, this sounds like a good plan, for Amnon follows Jonadab's directions to the letter.

Amnon is next in line to the throne and his health is of great importance, not only to his family, but also to all of Israel. Concerned, David hurries to Amnon's phony sick bed and, honoring Amnon's request, summons Tamar to care for her brother. Tamar is a good and obedient daughter; she arrives promptly and sets to work.

Tamar, like David, is not suspicious; both think only of Amnon's welfare. Tension builds, however, as the reader knows that Tamar is about to walk into a trap. As she kneads and then bakes little cakes for her brother, Amnon is thinking ahead. Like a cranky sick person, Amnon refuses to eat the food she proffers, and in agitation sends everyone, presumably servants and other royal attendants, from the room (2 Sam. 13:9). He asks Tamar to feed him the cakes in his bedchamber and she innocently complies. We can almost hear the informed reader shouting a warning to Tamar but, sadly, Tamar is drawn into Amnon's lair.

Once he has her where he wants her, he issues a detestable command that highlights their sibling relationship: "Come lie with me, my sister!" (2 Sam. 13:11). The text repeatedly uses familial designations (father, brother, sister) as a way to emphasize that trouble is brewing within the house (family) of David. While some scholars assert that Amnon's use of the word "sister" is a term of endearment, a euphemism for one's beloved, as in the Song of Solomon (4:9–12; 5:1–2), it is more likely the author's way of emphasizing the dual crimes (rape and incest) about to take place. Further, the fact that Tamar cleverly responds by using the term, "brother" to address Amnon seems to support this. Remaining calm, she appeals to Israel's strict moral code in hopes of bringing Amnon to his senses: "No, my brother, do not force me; for such a thing is not done in Israel; do not do anything so vile!" (2 Sam. 13:12). Surely, there is no "love banter" going on here, for Amnon's assault is premeditated, a fact that makes his crime even more heinous.

Like any woman in her position, Tamar is terrified. Her attacker is stronger than she, and Tamar must rely on her wits.

She quickly points out the negative consequences of Amnon's actions for them both: "As for me, where would I carry my shame? And as for you, you would be one of the scoundrels in Israel" (2 Sam. 13:13). Her argument makes a great deal of sense, for she is a virgin and he, a future king. Moreover, a deflowered princess and rapist prince would bring shame to the entire family.

When both arguments fail, Tamar switches tactics, urging Amnon to do the right thing and ask King David for permission to marry her. There is strict legislation forbidding marriage and sex between siblings (Lev. 18:9, 11; 20:17; Deut. 27:22), and rape is considered a capital crime (Deut. 22:23–24; 28–29). But, perhaps they can circumvent the law. If they were permitted to marry, Amnon would be able to satisfy his sexual desires whenever he wished. But of course, rape is not about sex; it is about power and control.

However, is Tamar's suggestion of marriage feasible, even attempting to circumvent the law? Are siblings permitted to marry under any circumstances? This calls into question the dating of the material found in 2 Samuel and the legal-moral code found in the Torah. Some scholars argue that 2 Samuel predates the rules laid out in the Torah and that there is precedent for brother-sister marriages in the ancient Near East—for example, Egyptian royals regularly married their siblings. Others argue that there are prohibitions in place against incestuous unions, but that royals, like Tamar and Amnon, are not bound by the same laws as the rest of the people and would be permitted to wed, should King David approve.

These are complex issues and the debate surrounding the dating of this material cannot be settled here. While addressing the question of whether or not siblings can wed may be germane insofar as Tamar's struggle to dissuade her brother from raping her is concerned (for she would not be the first victim to try just about anything to save herself from being sexually assaulted), the larger point is that raping one's sister is criminal, before and after the Torah injunctions are composed expressly forbidding it. The author knows this, Tamar knows this, and so does Amnon. But Amnon, like his father, sees, wants, schemes, and takes. Ignoring Tamar's sound reasoning and pleas for restraint, Amnon overpowers his sister and rapes her (2 Sam. 13:14).

Following the attack, Amnon, is "seized with a very great loathing" for his victim and orders her to "Get out!" (2 Sam. 13:15). Curiously, Tamar pleads: "No, my brother; for this wrong in sending me away is greater than the other that you did to me" (2 Sam. 13:16). Why does Tamar feel that banishment is adding insult to injury? Scholars typically assume that Tamar is referring to Deuteronomy 22:28–29, a law that requires the rapist to marry his victim and to pay her father a fine of fifty shekels for having raped his daughter.

Contemporary readers are likely horrified at such a law, for what woman wants to become the wife of her rapist? And why is the woman's *father* awarded the fifty shekels? During this time period, however, rape is understood only as a sexual crime, a crime of lust, and one that indicates a lack of restraint on the part of the rapist. The ancient laws did not take into account the psychology of rape, nor the resultant physical and emotional scars of the victim. Hence, Tamar and others like her would be considered social outcasts.

The father of a rape victim would have a difficult time marrying off his daughter; thus, the financial redress is awarded to him. As outrageous as it may seem, the only hope for a victim is to wed her rapist, and Tamar knows that this is her only hope as well. While many of the women stories in the Bible feature strong and capable women, who rise from the ashes, Tamar's story reminds us of a harsher reality. Women during biblical times are viewed as inferior to men, they are vulnerable, and regularly victimized by a system that does not regard their humanity as equal with that of their male counterparts.

Tamar's pleas to Amnon to refrain from banishing her are ignored in the same way he ignores her reasoned arguments against raping her in the first place. He callously orders a servant to remove her and lock her out of his bedroom. Once again, he fails to do the right thing. In fact, throughout the story, Amnon always does the wrong thing.

As in the story of David and Bathsheba, the author skillfully contrasts the actions of two characters; one who has power with another who does not. In 2 Samuel 11, it is the cuckolded husband of Bathsheba, Uriah the Hittite, the noble solider, who does all the right things, contrasted with David, the powerful king of Israel, who does the wrong things. Here, we have Tamar, a loving sister, who nurses her sick brother—the right thing to do—contrasted with Amnon, the dynastic heir-apparent, who does the wrong things, sexually assaulting his sister and then banishing her. In both cases, the victims in these stories are destroyed. Under David's direction, Uriah is purposely placed on the front line of battle and killed, while Tamar suffers a social death, doomed to forever live as a pariah among her people.

As if all of this is not enough, there is more suffering still. Tamar leaves her brother's bedchamber and makes public her personal humiliation. Engaging in Israel's traditional acts of mourning, she tears her long robe (the customary garment worn by virgin princesses), puts ashes on her head, and sobs aloud (2 Sam. 13:19). Her brother, Absalom, comes to console her and takes her into his home, and this is the last we hear of Tamar. But, her story does not end here. Her rape sets off an avalanche of bloodletting as the sword consumes David's house.

When King David hears of Amnon's crime, he is angry, but fails to punish him, "because he loved him, for he was his first-born" (2 Sam. 13:21). Like David's crime against Bathsheba, Amnon thinks he has skirted the consequences of his actions, but as always there is a price to be paid. Because David does the wrong thing and shirks his duty as a parent, Absalom is forced to punish Amnon. Echoing the belief that revenge is a dish best served cold, Absalom waits for two years before punishing Amnon. He throws a party and when Amnon is sufficiently intoxicated, Absalom orders his servants to kill the rapist (2 Sam. 13:27–29).

Revenge exacted, Absalom flees Jerusalem, only to return three years later to mount a rebellion against his own father. Absalom is killed during a battle against David's forces, when his long hair gets tangled between two trees. Interestingly, it is Joab, David's commander, who carried out the execution of Uriah the Hittite (2 Sam. 11:16–17), who runs Absalom through with the sword as he helplessly dangles, ensnared between the trees (2 Sam. 18:13).

The story of Tamar continues the cycle of abuse-of-power stories punctuating Israel's historical books, detailing the rise and fall of the monarchy (1–2 Sam.; 1–2 Kings; 1–2 Chron.). She is a tragic figure, inexorably linked to Bathsheba, for both are victims of premeditated sexual crimes involving the house of David. Both women pay a terrible personal price for the sins of their violators and both suffer the consequences of God's punishment of David. While we cannot help but draw parallels between Bathsheba and Tamar, there are also some significant differences. Although she begins as David's pawn, Bathsheba learns to work within the male dominated world of palace intrigue. She undergoes a remarkable transformation, from victim to victor, triumphantly securing the throne for her son, Solomon. Initially a mute victim, Bathsheba finds her voice and regains her personal power, thus becoming a respected queen.

Not so with Tamar. For her, there will be no metamorphosis, no transformation, and no triumphs, for Tamar is utterly destroyed by Amnon's crime. In an instant, she moves from virgin princess to rape victim. At the end of her story, she is sequestered away in the home of her doomed brother, Absalom, her royal robes torn asunder. She simply fades from the pages of Scripture, a sad casualty of the devouring sword within the house of David.

Tamar's Enduring Lessons

In the Bible, the woman-as-victim stories share several important elements. Understanding these elements helps to draw Tamar's story into sharper focus. The pattern goes something like this: The woman is victimized by a powerful man (or men), most often from within their own family, and the crime usually has a connection to sexuality. Generally speaking, there are two types of women-as-victim stories. The first features a female victim who somehow overcomes tragedy only to emerge victorious, like Bathsheba and Susanna. The story of Tamar represents the other, more dismal category. In such stories, the victim is completely destroyed, suffering a physical death (as in the tragic tale of the concubine in Judges 19, who dies after being brutally gang-raped by the local men of Gibeah) or a social death (like Tamar). The first category is hopeful, the second, hopeless.

It is the hopelessness associated with Tamar's tragedy that is the most salient feature of her story. It reveals to us the uncomfortable truth we are often afraid to admit: that sometimes, there are events and circumstances from which we cannot fully recover. We are told, and we like to believe, that everyone—through attitude adjustment, therapy, prayer, love, determination, or the gift of time—can bounce back from misfortune. Armed with this belief, in times of adversity, we struggle to find the right path that will lead us back to wholeness. We may learn to cope, but often the person who emerges bears little resemblance to our former selves. And, while most of us do find our way home, others remain hopelessly lost. Like Tamar, who disappears into her brother Absalom's home and from the pages of the Bible, the stark reality is that sometimes, we *do not* bounce back. Indeed, there are just some tragedies that exceed our ability to traverse them. Thus, the most enduring lesson Tamar's story offers us is a sober one.

Though suffering is an inevitable part of life, Tamar's suffering comes about through no fault of her own. She is, after all, simply a sister sent on a mercy mission to tend to an ailing sibling. While suffering due to one's own foolishness, ignorance, or self-indulgence is difficult to bear; suffering at the hands of another is unbearable. And, what happens to Tamar is unbearable.

Tamar begins as the beautiful, intelligent, privileged daughter of King David—but is quickly brought to ruin by the men in her family. In a horrible irony, her father and brother, two men who should love and protect her, are instead responsible for her devastation. And while few of us transgress to the degree of Amnon, Tamar's plight alerts us to the fact that our behavior, in word and deed, has the potential to profoundly affect the lives of others, even when we may not recognize it. For better or for worse, a parent's neglect, a teacher's sincere words of praise, or an inspiring sermon can change lives. Tamar's victimization teaches us to be more aware, more measured, and to simply appreciate the way in which our behavior impacts those around us.

When we think of Tamar, two images typically come to mind. The first features a young woman tenderly making heart-shaped cakes for her sick brother. We can almost see her, brow furrowed, kneading, baking, and proudly serving her curative fare. The second image is that of a woman in great pain, traumatized, and broken, she staggers from the scene of her rape in search of consolation. Fortunately, she finds the consolation she so desperately needs in her brother, Absalom.

Absalom's love and support, compared to Amnon's crime and David's neglect, paints a contrasting family portrait. Tamar's tale reminds us that families—then and now—are complicated, a source of comfort and consternation, joy and misery. We often rely on our family for emotional, physical, and spiritual support and when these needs are not met, or worse, when there is blatant abuse, the effects can be devastating and long-lasting.

Within families, for a variety of reasons, there are certain people—for example, grandparents, siblings, cousins—with whom we forge deeper relationships because we feel a closer connection to them. Absalom and Tamar seem to have this special connection. It is their relationship that is the one glimmer of hope in this otherwise tragic tale.

This glimmer is manifest in several actions. Absalom comforts Tamar and brings her into his home, where she presumably remains for the rest of her life. He even names his daughter after her, an endearing and tender gesture not to be overlooked. And, our modern views of "biblical justice" aside, Absalom punishes Amnon for his crime, something that David fails to do.

Absalom's revenge reminds us of another rape-revenge story, the one involving Dinah, the daughter of Jacob (Gen. 34). When Shechem, a local tribal chieftain, rapes Dinah, their sister, the sons of Jacob initially make nice. They even go so far as to promise marriage between the two (as prescribed in Deut. 22:28–29), providing that all the males in the tribe submit to circumcision, which they do. As they recover from their surgery, however, Jacob's sons attack and kill them. While this story is often viewed more in terms of the sons' abuse of the sacred covenant of circumcision, it is nonetheless clear that the brothers' intention is to avenge their sister's rape (Gen. 34:27, 31). And clearly, revenge is also on Absalom's mind.

Though some scholars are quick to point out that Absalom's political ambition may the reason behind the murder of Amnon, the author seems to contradict this notion: "Absalom hated Amnon, because he had raped his sister Tamar" (2 Sam. 13:22). Amnon's shiftless friend, Jonadab, the creator of the "pretend-to-be-sick-so-you-can-rape-your-sister plan," also confirms Absalom's true intentions when he speaks to David following Amnon's death: "This has been determined by Absalom [the revenge killing of Amnon] from the day Amnon raped his sister Tamar" (2 Sam. 13:32).

Following her rape, Tamar is described as "a desolate woman" (2 Sam. 13:20). We can imagine that Absalom's unwavering allegiance to his sister, his acknowledgment of the wrong done to her, and his desire to avenge her rapist, comforted Tamar in her desolation. While we can question Absalom's methods, and the not-so-rosy picture of him to follow, the fact remains; he is on Tamar's side during what are surely the darkest days of her life.

11

The Shunammite Woman: Volunteer

A Womb with a View

(1 Kings 4:8–31; 8:1–6)

One day Elisha was passing through Shunem, where a wealthy woman lived, who urged him to have a meal. So whenever he passed that way, he would stop there for a meal. She said to her husband, "Look, I am sure that this man who regularly passes our way is a holy man of God. Let us make a small roof chamber with walls, and put there for him a bed, a table, a chair, and a lamp, so that he can stay there whenever he comes to us."

One day when he came there, he went up to the chamber and lay down there. He said to his servant Gehazi, "Call the Shunammite woman." When he had called her, she stood before him. He said to him, "Say to her, Since you have taken all this trouble for us, what may be done for you? Would you have a word spoken on your behalf to the king or to the commander of the army?" She answered, "I live among my own people." He said, "What then may be done for her?" Gehazi answered, "Well, she has no son, and her husband is old." He said, "Call her." When he had called her, she stood at the door. He said, "At this season, in due time, you shall embrace a son." She replied, "No, my lord, O man of God; do not deceive your servant." The woman conceived and bore a son at that season, in due time, as Elisha had declared to her (2 Kings 4:8–17).

WEALTHY, independent, and a respected member of the community, the nameless woman from Shunem represents a unique type of female biblical character. Though most unnamed women in the Bible are identified in terms of a close male relation (for instance, *Noah's* wife or *Jephthah's* daughter), the Shunammite Woman is identified in relation to her town, a biblical convention sometimes used in stories featuring rich, socially prominent women. Her story appears in the cycle of tales associated with the enigmatic prophet, Elisha, with whom she forges a close personal relationship.

Included in the books of Kings, the Elijah-Elisha tales are filled with heroic actions, fantastic miracles, and prophetic pronouncements. The story of the Shunammite and Elisha closely parallels the tale of the Widow of Zarephath and Elijah (1 Kings 17). Both women offer hospitality to a prophet and are subsequently the recipients of prophetic miracles. Elijah lives with the Widow of Zarephath during a famine and not only makes a days worth of flour and oil last for an entire year, but also restores life to her dead son (1 Kings 17). Elisha stays at the home of the barren Shunammite, bestows the gift of a child to her, and later raises that son from the dead.

Biblical scholar Tikva Frymer-Kensky (See Resources), among others, discusses the Shunammite's story in terms of a three-act play. Each act contains a miracle, which builds upon the other, and serves to illuminate the power of the prophet. Act one (2 Kings 4:8–17) develops the relationship between the prophet and his pious patroness, culminating in the miracle of a son. Act two (2 Kings 4:18–37) describes the death and miraculous resurrection of the son. The final act (2 Kings 8:1–6) takes place much later, with the restoration of the Shunammite's property seized by the king during a famine. The land is returned to her (miracle number three) because the king is so impressed with the stories he has heard about Elisha's resurrection abilities (miracle number two).

Act one begins with a building project. Elisha travels regularly to Shunem on prophetic business and dines at the home of the hospitable Shunammite Woman and her husband. Recognizing him as "a holy man of God" (2 Kings 4:9), she decides to build a small room for him on the roof of her home so that he may stay there during his visits. The guest room is the Shunammite's idea; she conceives of it and follows it through to fruition. We have no record of her husband's response to the proposal, the first indication that perhaps it is *she* who wears the pants in the family.

Lounging in his new room during one of his visits, Elisha tries to think of a way to show his appreciation for the Shunammite's hospitality. First, he offers to put in a good word to the king or army commander on her behalf. Apparently, Elisha has friends in high places. But so does the Shunammite and she declines his offer (2 Kings 4:13). The way in which Mrs. Shunammite rebuffs Elisha's offer is curious: "I live among my own people" (2 Kings 4:13). Some scholars suggest that the phrase, "I live among my own people" indicates a departure from the social custom of the day whereby a man and woman marry and settle down in the town or village of the *husband's* family. But, since most couples are from the same town, this does not make much sense. The more plausible explanation is that the Shunammite wishes to convey the fact that she is a woman of means, with her own connections and she certainly does not need out-of-town prophets to do her networking for her.

Elisha is stumped. How can he repay the Shunammite's kindness? Clueless, he turns to his trusted servant and sidekick, Gehazi, for suggestions. Gehazi points out what should be obvious: the Shunammite is barren. Though the barren woman motif is a common biblical theme, the Shunammite does not quite fit the pattern of other barren woman stories—that is, the condition of barrenness is revealed, followed by a prayer or intercession usually by the woman's husband to God for help, a birth is announced, and a son is born. In most of these tales, including the stories Sarah, Rebekah, Rachel, and Hannah, the woman is *defined* by her barrenness, but this is not the case with the Shunammite. She is defined instead by her relationship with the prophet.

Her barrenness becomes an occasion for a prophetic miracle, for when Elisha summons the Shunammite a second time, he promises her a son. Her reaction, however, is not what we might expect: "No, my lord, O man of God; do not deceive your servant" (2 Kings 4:16). Scholars have questioned the meaning of this and other aspects surrounding the bedroom conversation between Elisha and the Shunammite Woman.

For example, at first, Elisha does not speak directly to her, but through Gehazi ("Say to her. . ." 2 Kings 4:12) in what appears to be a biblical form of the game, *Telephone*. Does Elisha need an interpreter? Evidently not, for he and the Shunammite converse without the help of Gehazi just a few verses later. Perhaps, then, he wishes to lend a formal air to the proceedings, as Frymer-Kensky suggests, although surely it is a bit incongruous for a formal conversation to take place in the guest bedroom of one's benefactor. In either case, the Shunammite will have none of this. She bypasses Gehazi and responds directly to the prophet.

But, what can we conclude about the Shunammite's reaction to the prediction of a son? Does her statement, "No, my lord, O man of God; do not deceive your servant" (2 Kings 4:16) indicate disbelief or does her less-than-enthusiastic response mean that perhaps she does not want a child? The text is unclear, and perhaps the best way to understand the Shunammite's response is as an expression of incredulity. While the Shunammite may be skeptical, Elisha follows through on his promise, and just as predicted, the Shunammite gives birth to a son.

Act two begins as the text fast-forwards a few years and the son falls ill while working in the fields with his father. He is brought to his mother and dies in her arms (2 Kings 4:18–20). The Shunammite carries the child upstairs and lays him across the prophet's bed. Her motivation for doing this is unclear, but she may view this place as somehow holy. Maybe the bed has some curative powers that will revive her son? She leaves the child on the bed, and tells her husband to have a servant prepare a donkey for a trip to visit Elisha on Mount Carmel. Her husband seems confused but complies. Elisha spies her from a distance and is concerned, for the Lord has not revealed to him the reason for her trip (2 Kings 4:29). Ignoring the social protocols of her day, she pushes past Elisha's feeble sentry, Gehazi, and approaches the prophet, boldly challenging him: "Did I ask you for a son? Did I not say, 'Do not mislead me?'" (2 Kings 4:28).

She did not ask for a child, nor did she express the need or desire to have one. But now that she has him, she loves him and, like any parent, is consumed with fear, worry, and grief. It was Elisha's idea to give her a son and now he must help her. He seems to understand this and sends Gehazi ahead to help. But Gehazi is not who the Shunammite has in mind; her faith rests in Elisha. He alone can raise her son. She takes a stand and refuses to leave without the prophet, which proves to be a good move as Gehazi's attempts to revive the child fail.

Before Elisha performs his next miracle, we must take a moment to review this scene from within the framework of the strict patriarchal rules that regulate male-female interaction during biblical times. From the perspective of the ancient audience, Elisha is a well-known, powerful prophet who deserves to be treated with reverence and respect. And here we have a woman calling him to task and, essentially, ordering him around? Who does the Shunammite think she is, anyway? After all, this is the prophet who once released a pair of she-bears to maul a group of children who made fun of him (2 Kings 3:23–25). Clearly, he is not a man with whom one trifles. Yet, the Shunammite speaks to him like a peer, or in this case, almost like one of her servants, for she makes demands and expects him to acquiesce.

The story of the Shunammite represents an entirely different model of male-female social intercourse, one based on equality and friendship, something virtually unattested to in ancient Israel. The writer's purpose in presenting such a "modern" relationship between prophet and patroness is a way to highlight the veracity of Elisha's prophetic vocation. As a wealthy, powerful woman in her own right, the Shunammite offers trusted and authoritative testimony to Elisha's authenticity. Moreover, because the Shunammite is both a believer and a benefactor, she is rewarded with prophetic miracles. Hence, her devotion bolsters his credentials and turns him into a legendary figure that inspires us all.

Remember that the stories in the Bible, and in particular the women stories, are less about women and more about God. The prophet is God's spokesperson on Earth, hence, the Shunammite's faith in the prophet serves as a powerful example of how we should behave toward the prophet—and, ostensibly, toward God.

Now it is time for Elisha's most memorable miracle.

Elisha arrives at the home of the Shunammite and immediately goes up to the rooftop room where the initial prophecy of a son took place and where the dead child now lies. Interestingly, most resurrection stories in the Bible take place in an upper room or some other elevated place. For example, Elijah raises the dead son of the Widow of Zarephath in an upper room (1 Kings 17:21–24).

Elisha closes the door, prays, and in what seems almost like artificial respiration, the prophet places "his mouth upon his mouth, his eyes upon his eyes, and his hands over his hands" (2 Kings 4:34). Slowly, the little boy's body grows warmer; he wakes, and sneezes seven times. He is returned to his mother and the pair drops out of sight for several chapters.

The final act of the Shunammite's story takes place on the threshold of a seven-year famine. Elisha returns to the Shunammite and warns her to flee the impending catastrophe.

Having complete faith in the man who raised her son from the dead, she gathers her household and settles for seven years in the land of the Philistines. It is noteworthy that the prophetic warning of the famine is given to the *woman* of the house, rather than her husband. In fact, in all of act three (2 Kings 8:1–6), the author makes no mention of Mr. Shunammite. It is *her* household, *her* house, *her* land, and *her* son.

After the famine, the Shunammite returns to her hometown, only to find her land and home have been confiscated by the king, apparently a common practice during times of war or famine. We wonder if perhaps she now regrets Elisha's offer to put in a good word for her to the king (2 Kings 4:13). The Shunammite sets out to appeal to the king for the return of her property. As it turns out, at that very moment, Gehazi is regaling the king with prophetic miracle stories, featuring none other than the Shunammite's son. The king is particularly impressed with the resurrection miracle, for when the Shunammite arrives with her brought-back-from-the-dead-son, he grants her request. The curtain falls on this act with the complete restoration of the Shunammite's home and land, a third miracle, made possible through her beloved prophet, Elisha.

The Shunammite Woman's Most Enduring Lessons

The story of the wealthy woman from Shunem teaches us much about the nature of faith, unexpected gifts, and the importance of hospitality. These enduring lessons are framed within the context of the Shunammite's connection to Elisha. Theirs is an exclusive relationship that does not seem to include her husband. Given the socially restrictive, male-dominated culture of the day, it is highly unusual for a man to have any sort of relationship with a woman outside of his immediate family. While this sort of man-woman relationship is relatively unheard of in the patriarchal world of the Bible, there are rare exceptions, especially when a prophet is involved.

Recall, for example, the alliance formed between the prophet Nathan and Bathsheba (2 Sam. 11–12; 1 Kings 1–2), not to mention Elijah's relationship with the Widow of Zarephath (1 Kings 17:17–24).

The author focuses on the exclusivity of the woman-prophet friendship for, despite her wealth and social standing, she is still considered a second-class citizen. The prophetic concern for social justice, a unique movement in the dog-eat-dog world of the ancient Near East, is expressed in Elisha's egalitarian treatment of the Shunammite Woman. Treating others fairly is not only a prophetic theme, but also the cornerstone of Judeo-Christian moral teaching.

The relationship between the Shunammite and the prophet is presented as ideal, a model for the faithful to follow. This is not to say that their relationship is unattainable perfection; rather, what makes it exemplary is its complexity, the author's way of reminding us that the nature of faith itself is also complicated. Even when faith rests on sturdy shores, it is nonetheless subject to the tides. The Shunammite expresses this natural ebb and flow as she vacillates between trust and doubt in Elisha's powers.

For example, the Shunammite's response to the prophetic prediction of a son is ambivalent and there is no indication that she wants a child. Once the child is born, however, like most mothers, she falls in love. But then the child dies. This is not supposed to be part of the plan! The Shunammite confronts the prophet and demands that he raise her child, reminding him that, after all, the baby miracle was *his* idea. By the end of the story, when warned of the impending famine, she trusts the prophetic prediction and leaves her home without question.

Barrenness, a surprise pregnancy, the death of a child, and famine are formidable challenges for the Shunammite. Her struggles remind us that there are times, in every life, when we feel saddled with burdens that exceed our ability to carry them. We may feel overwhelmed by circumstance and unjustly singled out for a disproportionate share of life's challenges. An unexpected pregnancy, the loss of a career, the end of a marriage, and countless other unanticipated detours from the planned itinerary of our lives can plunge us into the abyss of uncertainty. We look around at the seemingly carefree lives of others with envy and wonder how we will manage.

But manage we do. And, over time, we may find that the very thing we did not want, the very thing we feared, or the awesome responsibility we were convinced we could not shoulder, turns out to be our greatest blessing. This certainly seems to be the case with the Shunammite and her son.

If the Shunammite's story teaches us something about fairness and faith, it also teaches us the value of hospitality. A dying virtue in Western culture, particularly in the United States, hospitality has been replaced with suspicion; and the milk of human kindness, with curdle of self-absorption. We spend our days working for the big house in which we can store our many things, and we spend most of our free time tending to and guarding our many possessions. Greed and consumption seem to be the hallmarks of modern living. While working hard and acquiring possessions is not intrinsically evil, we must be mindful to share our blessings with those less fortunate. The Shunammite opens her home to Elisha because she can afford to do so and because the prophet is a man of God. She shares her wealth with one who has very little, thus modeling the proper biblical attitude toward wealth and possessions.

In the ancient world, travelers were dependent upon the kindness of strangers. The scarcity of inns, coupled with the fact that most people could not afford to pay for their lodgings, made hospitality a social necessity. Even today, people in the Middle East are well-known for their friendliness and generosity. Wary tourists often misconstrue this timeless ethic and attribute ulterior motives to gestures of hospitality. While a measure of caution is always prudent—at home or abroad—the Shunammite's kindness inspires us to trust and to remain open to new friendships. What makes her story so memorable, in fact, is her generous spirit.

The Shunammite Woman is not merely a pious follower of a powerful holy man. Nor is her life simply an opportunity for Elisha to dazzle us with his miracles. She is first and foremost a dedicated and loving friend. The model of Middle Eastern hospitality, piety, and strength, the Shunammite Woman transcends the social and gender boundaries of her day and lives life on her own terms, becoming for us the prototype of a modern woman.

12

Susanna: Victim and Vindicator
Dirty Old Men
(Dan. 13)

Oㅤne day, while they were waiting for the right moment, she entered the garden as usual, with two maids only. She decided to bathe, for the weather was warm. Nobody else was there except the two elders, who had hidden themselves and were watching her. "Bring me oil and soap," she said to the maids, "and shut the garden doors while I bathe." They did as she said; they shut the garden doors and left by the side gate to fetch what she had ordered, unaware that the elders were hidden inside. As soon as the maids had left, the two old men got up and hurried to her. "Look," they said, "the garden doors are shut, and no one can see us; give in to our desire, and lie with us. If you refuse, we will testify against you that you dismissed your maids because a young man was here with you."

"I am completely trapped," Susanna groaned. "If I yield, it will be my death; if I refuse, I cannot escape your power. Yet it is better for me to fall into your power without guilt than to sin before the Lord." Then Susanna shrieked, and the old men also shouted at her, as one of them ran to open the garden doors. When the people in the house heard the cries from the garden, they rushed in by the side gate to see what had happened to her. At the accusations by the old men, the servants felt very much ashamed, for never had any such thing been said about Susanna (Dan. 13:15–27).

WHAT DO Andromeda, Rapunzel, Princess Leia, and Olive Oyl all have in common? Aside from their signature coifs, these seemingly disparate females have one other significant similarity: they are all, in one way or another, damsels in distress. Whether tied naked to a rock by a vengeful god, trapped in a tower by an evil witch, held captive by a depraved devotee of the dark side, or kidnapped by a corpulent paramour, Andromeda, Rapunzel, Princess Leia, and Olive Oyl are archetypes of a stock theme found in literature, opera, film, art, and even comic books.

Damsel stories are always the same: The woman, usually young and beautiful, is somehow rendered helpless and in need of male liberation. She cries out to the hero to save her, and before long, her hero arrives on a white horse—or drops from the sky in a red cape, or dons a kilt and paints his face blue—but arrive he does, sword drawn or fists poised, ready to rescue the fair lady from the clutches of evil.

The intriguing tale of Susanna, the beautiful, young, Jewish woman who is falsely accused of adultery only to be rescued from the death penalty by Daniel, is the Bible's version of a damsel in distress tale. But, if you're flipping though your Bible in search of Susanna's story and having a difficult time locating it, it may be that your Bible does not include her story at all. If all of this seems confusing, let's take a moment to address the story of Susanna itself and its placement within the biblical canon—a question almost as interesting as the story itself.

Susanna's story is an addition to the book of Daniel in the Greek translations of the Hebrew Bible. The book of Daniel is comprised of a series of short narratives and apocalyptic visions featuring Daniel, a pious young Jewish man living in exile in Babylon. The general focus of the book of Daniel is instructive—teaching Jews to hold fast to their faith in the face of foreign domination (at the time, Israel was a far-flung province of the Roman Empire) and to resist the polluting influences of other (above all, Roman) religions.

Most scholars agree that Susanna's saga, written in Hebrew, was appended to some translations of the book of Daniel around 100 B.C.E. This may seem problematic, given that this would place the story long after the events of the Babylonian captivity in which it is set (587–539 B.C.E). What may at first seem to be a glaring aberration, however, is in fact a fairly common biblical convention. Many, if not *most*, of the stories found in the Bible were written long after the purported events took place, sometimes even hundreds of years later.

But while Susanna's tale is accepted as part of the official canon by Catholics, and is included in the Apocrypha of many Protestant Bibles, it plays no role in the Jewish canon. Even so, official or not, Susanna is admired as a paragon of Jewish faith and fidelity.

What do we mean when we speak of the Apocrypha? The Apocrypha—which means "hidden" or "esoteric"—refers to a certain set of ancient Jewish religious documents that first emerged in the final centuries before the Common Era, in the Greek translation of the Jewish Bible produced in Alexandria, Egypt (called the *Septuagint*). The Apocrypha, in some editions of Christian Bibles, are included between the Old and New Testaments. Catholics call some of the Apocrypha *Deuterocanonical* or "secondarily canonical." Among others, the Apocrypha include such texts as Tobit, 1–2 Maccabees, Wisdom of Solomon, Judith, and additions to the book of Daniel, including the story of Susanna. For our purposes, we will refer to the Catholic version of Susanna as part of the book of Daniel—Daniel chapter 13, taken from the New American Bible (NAB). While the Catholic version of the story does not vary much from the Protestant account found in the Apocrypha, it nonetheless offers us the opportunity to read an alternative translation.

Not to be confused with what is "apocryphal," which refers to any document of an esoteric nature, the Apocrypha includes a variety of gospels, apocalypses, legends, and doctrines held in high regard among early Jews and Christians, though not part of anyone's "official" Bible. Some of these books have been known for centuries, such as the Infancy Gospel of Thomas with its tales about Jesus' childhood miracles, while other texts were only recently discovered, including the Dead Sea Scrolls (the term used for Jewish documents found in caves in the Judean Desert in 1947). Armed with this very basic understanding of the placement of Susanna's story within the canon—that it's included in the main text of the Catholic Bible, in the Protestant Apocrypha, and not included in the Jewish Hebrew Bible—let's explore this captivating tale of deception, faith, and heroism.

The story, which takes place in Babylon, begins almost like a fairy tale: The beautiful and pious young Susanna marries Joakim, a wealthy and respected member of the exilic community, and lives in a lovely home, surrounded by friends and family. For all intents and purposes, it would seem that she lives "happily ever after." As in most fairy tales, however, the story here soon takes a drastic turn with the entry of the villain, or in this case, villains.

The author specifically dwells on Susanna's beauty and piety—both of which were revered and respected in the ancient world. For beauty is a sign of God's favor, while religious devotion ("fearing the Lord" in Bible-speak) represents the correct model of behavior for all Jews. Of course, then as now, beauty often elicits a variety of unwelcome sexual advances and, as we shall see, Susanna's religious convictions allow the villains a point of entry.

It is at the home of her husband, Joakim, that all of the action unfolds. Joakim's home, which includes a garden, also serves as the local courthouse—two details important to the story. Modern readers might wonder why, if Susanna and Joakim are married, the author insists upon referring to the house and garden as belonging specifically to Joakim, as if Susanna is a mere guest or interloper. Considered the property of men, however, women rarely owned anything in their own right, so the designation of the home and garden as belonging to Joakim is not at all unusual.

Taking notice of Susanna during her daily walks in the garden, two elders (or court officials) who frequent Joakim's house become consumed with lust for her. It is clear from the outset of the story that the magistrates are the villains of the tale, for the Lord himself condemns them:

> That year, two elders of the people were appointed judges, of whom the Lord said: "Wickedness has come out of Babylon: from the elders who were to govern the people" (Dan. 13:5).

Suppressing their consciences and forsaking their scared duty to uphold the law, the elders turn away from the Lord until they are "overwhelmed with passion" for Susanna (Dan. 13:9–10). Initially, each elder keeps his desire to seduce Susanna to himself, but eventually they confide in one another and form an unholy sort of alliance (Dan. 13:10–14). Then, together, they wait for an opportunity to find her alone. They need not wait long, as it turns out. Bathing innocently in her garden one afternoon, Susanna has no idea that the men have hidden themselves in order to watch her. And when she sends her maids away to close the garden gates and to fetch oil and soap for the bath, the elders seize the opportunity, offering her an appalling choice:

> "Look, the garden doors are shut, and no one can see us. We are burning with desire for you; so give your consent, and lie with us. If you refuse, we will testify against you that a young man was with you and this was why you sent your maids away" (Dan. 13:20–21).

If she gives in to their demands, she will be violating the Lord's commandment against adultery—an offense punishable by death (Lev. 20:10; Deut. 22:22). If she refuses, they will falsely accuse her and, because they are "respected" elders and Susanna is a woman (in biblical times, a woman's testimony was considered unreliable in court proceedings), the magistrates will likely prevail. Nonetheless, Susanna's Jewish upbringing (Dan. 13:2) has taught her that there can be only one choice: She will *not* submit (Dan. 13:22–23). Instead, she cries out to her servants—while the elders shout even louder. When the servants rush to the garden to investigate the source of the commotion, the elders tell their concocted tale and the servants feel "very much ashamed, for nothing like this had ever been said about Susanna" (Dan. 13:27).

A trial is held the next day and a modestly veiled Susanna appears in court to face her accusers. Her parents, children, and other assorted relatives stand with her, weeping, but curiously absent from the throng of supporters is her husband, Joakim. No reason for his absence is given and we can only speculate: Did Joakim recuse himself from the proceedings because of his personal involvement with the defendant? Was he too distraught to watch the proceedings? Or, does his absence indicate that perhaps he himself believes Susanna is guilty? The text does not explain the case of the missing husband, and only when Susanna is finally exonerated, at the end of the story, does Joakim reappear (Dan. 13:63).

Acting as both prosecuting attorneys and judges, the elders order Susanna to remove her veil "so that they might feast their eyes on her beauty" (Dan. 13:32). In an alternative translation of this story found in the Septuagint—the Greek translation of the Hebrew Bible—Susanna is forced to remove *all* of her clothing and stand naked in front of the court. The magistrates testify that they saw Susanna with a young lover who fled before they could apprehend him and that Susanna refused to identify the phantom suitor (Dan. 13:36–41). Susanna is never given the opportunity to defend herself, and no one steps forward on her behalf. Thus, the assembly accepts the elders' testimony and Susanna is condemned to death. Upon hearing her sentence, Susanna cries out to God for rescue—and, as always in the Bible, when one cries out to the Lord, there is a response (Dan. 13:44–45). Here God sends a young boy, Daniel, to save Susanna from her unjust punishment.

Daniel confidently takes charge of the proceedings and shrewdly interrogates the elders separately, asking each to describe the alleged love nest. One asserts that the union took place under a mastic tree and the other, under the evergreen oak (Dan. 13:54–58). Daniel immediately recognizes the discrepancies in their stories, thereby proving their guilt (Dan. 13:51–59). And the men get exactly what they deserve—the death sentence originally handed down to Susanna (Dan. 13:47–62). Notwithstanding a little capital punishment, the story finally ends "happily ever after" with everyone praising God and Daniel.

Susanna's Enduring Lessons

At first glance, Susanna's story might strike us as simply a folktale that cleverly employs the well-known literary motif of the damsel in distress. But to read the story this way would miss the deeper meanings—and lessons—the anonymous author sought to impart. Perhaps the most obvious lesson is that *things are not always as they seem.*

On the surface, in many ways, Susanna represents the secret longings of many women, then and now. She seems to have it all—beauty, faith, friends and supporters, a loving family, and a rich husband. Who could ask for more? Of course, the reality is that physical beauty is ephemeral and that faith is often sorely tested by life's injustices and many sorrows. Friends sometimes let us down, families squabble, and spouses disappoint us (even rich ones!). Ironically, the very circumstances that should be a source of blessings turn out to be the cause of her misery.

Susanna's beauty, no doubt, captivated her husband, Joakim—but it also attracted the notice of the villains. Just as her wealth and social standing offered her the freedom to leisurely stroll daily through the garden, it also becomes the means of her entrapment. And, if her loved ones stand beside her in her trial, they nevertheless fail to step forward on her behalf. Finally, as already noted, her wealthy husband effectively abandons her, leaving her to face her would-be rapists, a publicly humiliating trial, and a death sentence, alone.

Above and beyond all of this is the question of Susanna's faith; for here is the primary lesson of the story. Through Susanna's plight, we learn, among other things, the importance of holding on to one's faith, even in the direst of circumstances. We also learn that faith is a lifelong commitment. Susanna's parents raised her to "fear God" and her faith seems central to her life. As with her beauty, it is Susanna's deep faith, ironically, that delivers her into this predicament even as it delivers her *out* of it as well. For had she given in to the elders, the whole affair would have been a source "only" of personal humiliation for Susanna, rather than an occasion for the death penalty.

Such unwavering faith can only prompt us to examine our own. Are we faithful because we feel sustained and renewed by it, or is our faith a more reflexive thing, simply going through the motions? Do we practice a particular religion because it is the religion that was handed down to us, or have we explored our religious tradition fully and freely choose it? Moreover, have we engaged in a genuine search for meaning—to really *know* God, rather than to simply *know about* God?

This story also emphasizes the central truth of God's enduring love and presence in our lives—even when we may not recognize it. This is perhaps best illustrated in the long and cherished biblical tradition that stresses the imperative of the afflicted to call out to God for rescue. For it is the very act of voicing one's grief, fear, or pain, it would seem, that moves God to respond. God's response always comes in the form of a deliverer: The people cry out to God from the shackles of Egyptian slavery, and God sends Moses to free them (Exod. 2:23–24). A barren woman, Hannah, cries out to the Lord for a son, and God blesses her with a baby boy, the great prophet, Samuel (1 Sam. 1:9–20). And so it is that Susanna also cries out to God for rescue from an unjust death sentence and God sends Daniel to save her.

The point of the "crying out" motif would seem to embody the biblical notion of "ask and you shall receive." We may not always believe that God hears our prayers and we may despair, believing that our predicament is beyond repair. And, while we ourselves may not experience a Moses or Daniel-type hero, God does respond to our cry, but often not in the way we might expect. God's help may come in the form of a book we happen to pick up or a film we watch that inspires us. Sometimes, God sends others to the rescue—often people we might not expect— as when a co-worker offers a surprisingly apt word of wisdom or encouragement, just when we need it most, or the person standing in line behind you in the bank gives you the balm of an unprompted smile. So, perhaps the challenge is for us to imagine God's work as broader in scope and remain open to the many ways in which God saves.

These same lessons were critically important to the post-exilic Jewish community from which Susanna's story comes. Indeed, the struggles to maintain Jewish identity and faith under Greek rule were challenges that faced the community, and although in this story the threat to the community happens to come from within, the subtext stresses obedience to God's law no matter *what* the circumstances. Thus, Susanna's steadfast faith serves as a model for all those who struggle to maintain their faith in a world that is increasingly riddled with pain and suffering.

Concluding Thoughts

A S WE CONCLUDE our study of twelve of the most intriguing women of the Hebrew Bible, it seems appropriate to take stock and to summarize what we have learned. Are there connections or general lessons we can glean from the lives of the twelve that might be helpful as we move forward?

We began our journey with a brief exploration of the world of the ancient Near East, examining the complex tapestry that sets the stage for the women stories in the Hebrew Bible. This tapestry, though arguably incomplete, reveals much about the way women lived, worked, cared for their families, and worshiped their God. And thanks to the pioneering efforts of archaeologists, biblical scholars, and historians, we have learned much about the daily lives of women during the first millennium.

As we read the women stories in the Hebrew Bible, however, we glimpse the underside of this unfinished tapestry. The knots, the various lengths and shades of thread, are like the women stories themselves, for while each thread is unique, it also contributes to the collective whole, the masterpiece that is the Hebrew Bible.

The sections of this book (Lovers, Liars, and Lawbreakers; Victims, Volunteers, and Vindicators) helped to loosely categorize the types of women in each story. These, of course, are not the only kinds of women stories in the Hebrew Bible, for there are tales of women as prophets, women as wisdom figures, judges, and scores more. The sections, however, helped alert us to the fact that there are indeed certain "type stories" associated with most female biblical figures. As we explored the various types of stories, we noted that many of the stories were not limited to just one type, but crossed over to offer a variety of insights and connections.

Some of the most common themes found in the twelve stories and most of the other women stories in the Bible surround issues pertaining to family, faith, and the land. Consequently, these are among the most common concerns in Judaism. For example, Susanna (Dan. 12) is a pious Jewess who would rather die then betray her religious convictions. Her story then is primarily a story about faith alone. Other stories, indeed most women stories, incorporated two or more of these themes. For example, Rebekah the mother of Jacob and Esau, like all the matriarchs, experiences a period of barrenness until the Lord blesses her with twin sons (Gen. 15:21–26). The catch is that only one of the sons, Jacob, is to continue the promise God made to Abraham. After receiving a powerful oracle from the Lord to this effect, Rebekah makes it her life's mission to see that Jacob prevails over Esau (Gen. 25:23). Hence, her story is not only about family, but it is also about deep faith in the Lord.

Rebekah's story reminds us of Bathsheba who, like Rebekah, works to make certain that her son, Solomon, will ascend to the throne ahead of his brother, Adonijah (1 Kings 1:15–28). Though her story is primarily about family, it is also about the faith and the land, for Solomon not only reigns with wisdom over the land, but he will also build the great Temple, dedicated to the Lord.

Likewise, the stories about Rahab and Ruth include all three themes of family, faith, and the land: The harlot, Rahab, who hides Joshua's spies in exchange for her family's preservation during the terrible Israelite siege of Jericho, is the first convert in the Promised Land (Josh. 2:11). And, Ruth, the loyal daughter-in-law who also professes faith in the God of Israel, migrates to the Promised Land from her native Moab, vowing loyalty and allegiance to her mother-in-law, Naomi (Ruth 1:14–19).

Another common theme among the twelve stories is "woman as savior or protector." Miriam protects her infant brother, Moses, when he is set adrift down the Nile. She watches him from the bulrushes and then puts forth Moses' own mother as a candidate to nurse him for his adopted mother, Pharaoh's daughter (Exod. 2:3–9).

In a very different type of tale, Delilah, the Philistine lover of Samson, protects her people when she betrays him (Judg. 16:15–21). Though she has been the recipient of scorn throughout the ages, Delilah actually saves her people from Samson's murderous rampages.

Other saviors include the wily Rebekah who saves Jacob from Esau's death threats (after Jacob steals Esau's blessing), by sending Jacob away to live with his Uncle Laban (Gen. 27:41–45). Rahab, who protects her family against the Israelite attack by cutting a deal with the Israelite spies (Josh. 2:12–13), and the Moabite, Ruth, who saves Naomi from starvation by gathering grain in Boaz's field (Ruth 2:17–18). Finally, the Shunammite Woman saves her son's life by summoning the prophet, Elisha, to revive him (2 Kings 4:30–36).

Though the women in these stories are themselves protectors and saviors, there are also stories in which powerful men save women. In the story of Ruth, Boaz becomes Ruth's protector, first against the unwanted advances of the field workers, and then, as her husband (Ruth 2:8–9; 4:10). As such, he also becomes Naomi's protector, for Ruth and Naomi are a "package deal."

In the story of Tamar, the sister of Absalom, her father, King David, fails to punish his son, Amnon, for raping her

(2 Sam. 13:21). The task of punishing Amnon falls to Absalom, and while Absalom's motives may have political undertones, he nonetheless seeks justice for his sister and has Amnon killed (2 Sam. 13:23–29). Absalom is also the one who takes his shamed and disgraced sister—victim-blaming is a sad reality in the world of biblical antiquity—into his home, where she presumably spends the rest of her life (2 Sam. 13:20). Finally, Daniel's brilliant defense of Susanna exonerates her from the false charges brought against her, thus saving her from the death penalty (Dan. 13:44–62).

Another central theme found in the women stories profiled in this book (and in the Hebrew Bible in general) is the concept of women as agents of change. The most obvious examples of women who herald something new are mothers who give birth to great sons. Rebekah gives birth to the future patriarch, Jacob (Gen. 25:26); Tamar gives birth to twins, Zerah and Perez, the latter of whom is included in David's genealogy (Gen. 38:27–30); Ruth gives birth to Obed, the grandfather of the great King David (Ruth 4:17); and Bathsheba becomes the mother of the future king and master builder, Solomon (2 Kings 12:24–25).

But, the agents of change are not limited to mothers. Some women, through their actions, usher in a new age for Israel. For example, Rahab stands at the threshold of Israel's occupation of the land. Her conversion and compliance with Joshua's spies allows for the destruction of the city of Jericho—the old regime—and makes room for the new: the people of Israel. Her actions allow God's chosen people to establish a firm foothold in the land promised to Abraham. In the same way, the Witch of Endor straddles a bygone era—the monarchy of the ineffective, tragically flawed King Saul—and the new era of the Davidic dynasty (1 Sam. 28:7–25).

The final similarity in the twelve stories has to do with women's ability to work within the confines of the oppressive androcentric, patriarchal system that limited so much of their power. Despite the suffocating social constraints that governed women's behavior, most of the women stories in the Hebrew

Bible feature clever females who somehow find a way to achieve their objective.

Accordingly, many of the women are classified as tricksters, for they often lie or manipulate others in order to achieve their ends. Rebekah is perhaps the best-known trickster who, along with her trickster son Jacob, fools the dying Isaac into bestowing his blessing on Jacob, rather than Esau, the rightful heir (Gen. 27).

A few chapters later, the widow Tamar dresses like a common harlot and tricks her father-in-law Judah into having sex with her so she that may have a child from his family—a right denied to her by her father-in-law (Gen. 38:12–18). During the Israelite captivity in Egypt, Miriam tricks Pharaoh's daughter into hiring (and paying) Moses' own mother to act as a wet nurse for her son (Exod. 2:7–9). When the people enter the Promised Land, Rahab lies to the Canaanite authorities regarding the whereabouts of Joshua's spies (Josh. 2:3–4), and sends them on a wild goose chase through the wilderness.

Delilah never lies, but she does manipulate Samson into revealing the secret of his superhuman strength. Her betrayal leads to his arrest and death but, as Samson dies, pulling down the two pillars of the Philistine temple between which he had been tied, he successfully kills over three thousand Philistines worshipping inside (Judg. 16:24–30). This means there are three thousand fewer Philistines with which Israel must contend.

Ruth, the girl who does all the right things, is nonetheless a seductress, who uses her feminine wiles to capture the heart of the wealthy Boaz (Ruth 3:7–11). Bathsheba makes certain her son's kingship is firm when she agrees to approach King Solomon on behalf of his rival, Adonijah, regarding Adonijah's desire to marry David's former nurse, Abishag. Bathsheba knows full well that Solomon would see this request as a threat to his throne and would be forced to eliminate the competition, once and for all (1 Kings 2:12–25).

Modern readers may wince when reading some of the trickster tales and feel that lying and manipulation is unethical, even sinful. But we must remember that, from the author's perspective, the trickster did what she had to do to bring about God's plan. This perennial concern supersedes the moral and ethical questions that arise regarding women (and men) tricksters. And, simply put, the ancient audience delighted in such tales in the same way that modern readers enjoy stories that feature the triumph of the underdog.

Though many of the twelve women stories share common themes and concerns, the characters themselves are quite distinct. Hebrew narrative prose is typically not very descriptive. It lacks certain details of time, place, and in-depth character analyses and instead presents a rather bare-bones version of events. Generally speaking, however, the women stories tend to be more developed and the characters themselves more complex.

Though women during biblical times were generally lumped together as someone's wife, mother, or daughter, the twelve women profiled in this book and, indeed, most of the women in the Hebrew Bible, are more than just a wife, mother, or daughter. They step out of these traditional roles to make a difference in the developing history of Israel. For example, among the twelve women presented in this volume, there is a harlot (Rahab), a prophetess (Miriam), two wealthy women (the Shunammite and Susanna), three royals (Bathsheba, Tamar, sister of Absalom, and Jezebel), and a medium (the Witch of Endor).

During a time when marriage was considered the normal state for adult males and especially adult females, three of the twelve women are single: Rahab, Delilah, and Miriam. And, while marriage and/or children are themes found in nearly half of the twelve stories (Rebekah, the widow Tamar, Ruth, Bathsheba, and the Shunammite), all of the marriages and families are unconventional by Israelite standards.

Rebekah's engagement to Isaac happens through the efforts of Abraham's chief steward (Gen. 27). While proxy engagements are not terribly unusual in the ancient world of arranged marriages, Rebekah's active role in the whole process is unique. Her brother and mother actually ask her to make up her own mind, an indication that Rebekah is a strong-willed woman, raised in a more egalitarian household than most women of her day (Gen. 27:57–59). She will also experience barrenness, until the Lord blesses her with twins and entrusts her to fulfill the chosen son's (Jacob) destiny (Gen. 25:21–26).

The widow Tamar, also the mother of twins, is impregnated in a most unconventional way (Gen. 38:13–19) and the Moabite, Ruth, who represents those dangerous foreign females forbidden by the straitlaced Torah legislators, vamps her way to marriage and motherhood (Ruth 3:7–11).

Bathsheba, the victim of David's uncontrolled passion, becomes pregnant with his child while she is still married to another man. Sadly, she suffers the loss of her firstborn son as part of David's punishment (2 Sam. 12:18). Finally, the Shunammite Woman does not seem to want a child at all. This lack of what is considered a fundamental desire in all women makes her wholly unique. The prophet, Elisha, gives her the gift of a son anyway and re-gifts the child when he raises him from the dead (2 Kings 4:16–17; 32–35).

Despite the fact that the women stories often share common themes, the uniqueness of the women characters presents us with a rather interesting paradox that very much speaks to the paradox of Israel as a whole. Though Israel is united by a common ethic and covenant with the elusive God of the universe, she is nonetheless a coat of many colors, unlike any other nation, or any other people.

As we turn to the title of this book, *Good Girls, Bad Girls*, it seems prudent to ask the question: What makes a good girl good and a bad girl bad? The simple answer to this question is: That depends on your point-of-view and who is telling the story. Of course, we are getting a rather biased view, for the victors usually write the stories in the Hebrew Bible, and more generally, history as a whole.

Composed by many authors over a long period of time, the Hebrew Bible is heavily edited and details the growing pains of a nation and her relationship with her God. While the women stories certainly reflect this reality, they are much more than a metaphor for Israel's emergence as a people and a nation. Viewed through the lens of the ancient authors, certain women are good and others bad; some *very* bad. The bad-girl stories are included in the canon because they are instructive, teaching us how *not* to behave, alerting us to the polluting influence of foreign cults, and reaffirming the veneration of the One True God.

From the author's perspective, among the twelve, there are really only two truly bad girls, Delilah and Jezebel. But are they really that bad? And can it be said that even the bad girls have some redeeming qualities? Delilah is viewed as a bad girl for two reasons: She is a foreigner and she betrays Samson, a man revered by the author as a great judge in Israel.

Jezebel is the Phoenician queen and wife of the equally evil King Ahab (1 Kings 16:31). Jezebel is bad because she is a foreigner but, unlike Delilah, Jezebel seeks to impose her religious beliefs on the people of Israel. She even goes so far as to attempt to eliminate the competition by attacking the prophets of the Lord (1 Kings 18:13). This, of course, elicits a harsh response from the prophet, Elijah, who retaliates and slaughters some 850 prophets of Baal and Asherah, Jezebel's beloved deities (1 Kings 18:40). Jezebel is also considered a villain because she practices social injustice when she has an innocent man killed and then seizes his land (1 Kings 21:8–14).

It is clear that the ancient writers feel that Delilah and Jezebel are patently evil. Viewed through a more contemporary lens, however, we might have a more sympathetic understanding. Delilah, after all, is a single gal who is under pressure from the local authorities to help them capture a terrorist. Viewed from the Philistine perspective, she might be considered a great heroine; but the Philistines did not write the story. Modern readers might understand that there are mitigating circumstances that influence her decision to betray Samson and that when all is said and done, Samson is hardly a paragon of virtue himself.

Jezebel is often cited as the bad girl extraordinaire in the Hebrew Bible. While Jezebel's actions certainly make her a contender for that title, the honor actually belongs to a woman not profiled in this book, Athaliah (2 Kings 8:18, 26; 11; 2 Chron. 21:6; 22–24). The only queen to have ruled over Israel/Judah in the entire Hebrew Bible, Athaliah is a paranoid and murderous ruler. Though her parentage is unclear, most sources cite either King Omri (2 Kings 8:26; 2 Chron. 22:2) or his son, King Ahab (2 Kings 8:18; 2 Chron. 21:6) as her father. If it is the latter, then her mother may be Jezebel, though the text does not expressly state this (she may be the daughter of another of Ahab's wives). Still, since Jezebel is painted as such an evil character in the Hebrew Bible, the apple-doesn't-fall-far-from-the-tree connection between the two villainous queens seems reasonable.

Athaliah assumes the throne after the death of her son, King Ahaziah, and she systematically slaughters members of the royal family who might attempt to wrestle the throne from her hands. One of her grandsons, Joash, escapes the bloodletting when his aunt, Jehosheba, hides him away in "the house of the Lord" (2 Kings 11:3). Athaliah rules for six years, until she is killed in a coup and the seven-year-old Joash assumes the throne (2 Kings 11:13–21).

Athaliah makes Jezebel seem somewhat tame by comparison. After all, Jezebel's actions are largely motivated by her religious convictions. Jezebel's miscarriage of justice regarding Naboth, however, is difficult to justify, even through a more contemporary, sympathetic reading. Moreover, unlike her contest with Elijah, her mistreatment of Naboth has nothing to do with her religious beliefs. In the author's estimation, Jezebel serves as terrible warning about the dangers of foreign wives and their odious gods.

Now, what about the good girls? What makes them truly good? Modern readers may have a different standard regarding what constitutes "good" behavior. For example, Rebekah is a celebrated biblical matriarch, despite the fact that she demonstrates favoritism among her children. She also lies, deceives, and manipulates her husband, Isaac, and son Esau. While the biblical authors admire such trickery in the context of bringing about God's plan, contemporary readers find such behaviors troubling.

Modern readers may also take issue with a prostitute who betrays her people and brings about their slaughter (Rahab) and a woman who dresses like a harlot to trick her father-in-law into having sex with her (the widow Tamar). Some might argue that these differences in perspectives between ancients and moderns muddy the waters, making it difficult to definitively state just who is really bad and who is truly good.

In the introduction to this book, I stated that in telling each story, I attempt to remain faithful to the thoughts, ideas, and intentions, as well as I may discern them, of the biblical author or authors. With this in mind, perhaps the question regarding who is bad and who is good is really the wrong question to ask. The differences in time, culture, and societal shifts in perspectives, especially regarding the status of women, make this question a difficult one. Perhaps the question ought to be: What is the ancient author trying to tell me? More specifically:

> What is the author trying to teach me about God?
> What is the author trying to teach me about myself?
> What is the author trying to teach me about others?

In asking such questions, it is helpful to recall some of the enduring lessons imparted to us by the twelve women profiled in this book. These lessons invite us to reflect upon the meaning of each story and the ways in which they can be helpful to us today.

Because a woman's primary role in the biblical world was to care for her family, most of the stories and therefore the lessons learned are set within the context of family. Rebekah, the second of the biblical matriarchs and the first woman featured in this book, receives a personal directive from the Lord that shapes her life; her thoughts, decisions, and actions are framed within the context of what God wants from her. Though Rebekah knows exactly what God wants from her, the rest of us are not so lucky. Discerning God's will, in most cases, is a difficult task. And even if we are successful in articulating what we *perceive* God wants from us, living our lives in accord with God's plan is, at best, challenging.

Like Rebekah, the widow Tamar must also work from within her family to bring about God's plan. Her story teaches us that, despite our best efforts, sometimes things do not turn out the way we planned. Twice widowed and denied her right to marry and have children within the family of Judah, Tamar reminds us that there are certain duties and expectations that exist within families, in this case, Judah's obligation to honor the law of levirate. Tamar's tenacity in reclaiming what is rightfully hers inspires us to abandon the mythology of the status quo and to demand justice, even from within the closed ranks of our own family.

The setting of Miriam's story features her as part of a larger wilderness family as well as part of a more intimate trio that includes her brothers, Moses and Aaron. It is this latter relationship that forms the core of the narrative about her. As such, Miriam's story speaks to the very nature of the sibling relationship which, in terms of intimacy, shared experience, and longevity, is unlike any other. Indeed, our relationship with our brothers and sisters is often the first relationship we form with people other than our parents and can impact the success or failure of all future relationships, both personal and professional.

A tragic tale of betrayal and rape, Tamar, sister of Absalom, is a sibling story of another sort. It serves, among other things, as a stark reminder that we are vulnerable and that there are certain events from which we may never fully recover. Absalom's devotion to his sister helps to mediate Tamar's desperate situation, for he protects her, takes her into his home and avenges her honor. His actions offer a spark of hope in this otherwise abysmal story for they speak to the power in each of us to console and to offer comfort to those near and dear to us.

But, it is not always someone from within our own family who reaches out to us in our hour of need. When King Saul learns that he and his sons will die the next day in battle, the Witch of Endor, who was banished from the land by Saul himself, emerges as a caring and consoling friend who offers sustenance and sympathy to the broken and bereaved king. Her compassion and kindness reminds us that we are called to extend mercy beyond the small circle of our family and friends—for we are all part of the greater family of God.

The Shunammite Woman recognizes this truth when she offers hospitality to Elisha, a man of God and prophet of the Lord. When her son dies, it is her friend Elisha who recognizes the depth of her sorrow and steps forward to ameliorate it. The Shunammite bears testimony to the saving actions of God, the power of the prophet, and the enduring love between friends.

The harlot Rahab offers hospitality, friendship, and protection to Joshua's spies. Her actions, like the Shunammite Woman's, are motivated by faith. She courageously hides Joshua's spies, lies to the authorities, and negotiates a deal that secures her family's safety. Her story is one of faith-inspired action, a common element in nearly all of the women stories in the Hebrew Bible.

This truth is most evident in the story of Susanna, whose picture-perfect life is shattered in an instant when she is accused of a crime she did not commit. While Daniel is featured as the hero who rescues Susanna from execution, it is actually her unwavering faith in God that saves her. Susanna's story calls us to examine the depth of our own faith: Is it real, or simply a matter of going through the motions? Rahab and Susanna teach us that faith saves. Faith enables us to endure suffering and uncertainty; it helps us to transcend our present circumstances, to live in hope, and to envision new realities.

This ability to grow, change, and to transcend our present circumstances is most manifest in the story of Bathsheba. Though she begins as the hapless victim of King David's lust, her remarkable transformation, from victim to powerful queen, offers us hope in our own struggles against injustice and victimization. On a smaller scale, her story teaches us to embrace the many changes, both good and bad, that come into our lives.

Ruth embodies the realties of change as she loses her husband, leaves her homeland, immigrates to a new country, remarries, and has a child. Through her love and continued devotion to Naomi, Ruth teaches us that change does not mean that we must discard or abandon the people, places, or things from our past. Indeed, Ruth's unwavering love and loyalty to her mother-in-law become part of her new life with Boaz and Obed.

While Ruth is known for her filial devotion and loyalty, she nonetheless leaves Moab, her family, and her people to begin a new life. Delilah, on the other hand, remains loyal to her own people. Her betrayal of Samson, when viewed within the context of tribal fidelity, offers us an alternative understanding of Delilah as a Philistine heroine who single-handedly rescues her people from a dangerous menace. This alternative understanding can likewise be applied to Jezebel who, in the estimation of the biblical authors, is the Queen of Mean. While it is difficult to excuse many of her actions, from a Phoenician perspective, Jezebel might be viewed as a woman of great religious convictions, for she holds fast to her faith in the face of extreme opposition.

The enduring lessons of the remarkable twelve women profiled in this book teach us much about God, ourselves, and others, but the lessons presented here are by no means the only lessons we can glean from these ageless tales. Each of us, at different stages of life, may discover new lessons that were missed during a previous reading of a particular story. This is one of the many reasons millions find comfort and hope in the

Bible, which has served as a perennial source of wisdom throughout the ages. And so, I encourage you to read and re-read these and other stories in the Bible, both for enjoyment and spiritual nourishment.

Through the sands of time, a hazy image appears beside a well. A hand beckons, a voice calls out a greeting, and we follow. Our guide takes us to a faraway place and time that is at once different, yet hauntingly similar to our own. As the image becomes more distinct, we recognize the face and see vestiges of our mothers, sisters, wives, daughters, friends, and ourselves.

To read the women stories in the Hebrew Bible is to enter into a relationship with the ancient women whose life-challenges are remarkably similar to our own, for they reflect the time-less concerns of children, family, work, and faith, common to every woman of every age.

As we read their stories, we cheer for their victories, mar-vel at their accomplishments, and commiserate in their sor-rows, as they speak to the heart of our own circumstances. We take comfort in the fact that the women who came before us have prepared us for our own journey, that path we tread is well-worn, tested, and fashioned with signposts along the way. The women of the Bible are our foremothers in faith, trailblaz-ers, who remind us that women are made in the likeness and image of God; they are powerful, resourceful, beautiful, and creative; for they are every woman.

Resources

Achtemeir, Paul J. *HarperCollins Bible Dictionary*. San Francisco: Harper San Francisco, 1996.

Akenson, Donald Harmon. *Surpassing Wonder: The Invention of the Bible and the Talmuds*. Chicago: University of Chicago Press, 1998.

Albright, William Foxwell. *Archaeology and the Religion of Israel*. 5th ed. Garden City, NJ: Doubleday, 1968.

———. *Yahweh and the Gods of Canaan: A Historical Analysis of Two Contrasting Faiths*. Winona Lake, IN: Eisenbrauns, 1990.

Alter, Robert. *The Art of Biblical Narrative*. New York: Basic Books, 1981.

———. *The David Story*. New York: W. W. Norton & Co., Inc., 1999.

Anderson, Berhard W. and Katheryn Pfisterer Darr. *Understanding the Old Testament*. 4th ed. Englewood Cliffs, NJ: Prentice Hall, 1998.

Armstrong, Karen. *A History of God*. New York: Knopf, 1993.

Berlin, Adele and Marc Zvi Brettler. *The Jewish Study Bible*. New York: Oxford University Press, 2004.

Belis, Alice Ogden. *Helpmates, Harlots, and Heroes: Women's Stories in the Hebrew Bible*. Louisville: Westminster/John Knox Press, 1994.

Blenkinsopp, Joseph. *The Pentateuch: An Introduction to the First Five Books of the Bible*. New York: Doubleday, 1992.

Boadt, Lawrence. *Reading the Old Testament: An Introduction*. New York: Paulist Press, 1984.

Boling, Robert G. and G. Ernest Wright. "Joshua." *Anchor Bible* 6. New York: Doubleday, 1982.

Bos, Johanna. "Out of the Shadows: Genesis 38; Judges 4:17–22; Ruth 3." *Semeia* 42 (1988): 37–67.

Broderick, Robert C., ed. *The Catholic Encyclopedia*. Nashville: Thomas Nelson, 1987.

Brown, Raymond E., Joseph Fitzmyer, and Roland E. Murphy, eds. *The Jerome Biblical Commentary*. Englewood Cliffs, NJ: Prentice-Hall, 1968.

Brueggemann, Walter. *Theology of the Old Testament: Testimony, Dispute, Advocacy*. Minneapolis: Fortress Press, 1997.

Burns, Rita. *Old Testament Message 3: Exodus, Leviticus, Numbers*. Wilmington, DE: Michael Glazier, Inc., 1983.

Bury, J. B., S. A. Cook, and F. E. Adcock, eds. *The Cambridge Ancient History: The Persian Empire*. Vol. 4. Cambridge: University Press, 1964.

Clifford, Richard, S. J. *Old Testament Message 4: Deuteronomy*. Wilmington, DE: Michael Glazier, Inc., 1989.

Coogan, Michael David, ed. *The New Oxford Annotated Bible with the Apocryphal/Deuterocanonical Books*. 3rd ed. New York: Oxford University Press, 2001.

Davies, Philip. *Scribes and Schools: The Canonization of the Hebrew Scriptures*. Louisville: Westminster/John Knox, 1998.

Deen, Edith. *All the Women of the Bible*. New York: Harper Collins, 1988.

Demers, Patricia. *Women as Interpreters of the Bible*. New York: Paulist Press, 1992.

Finkelstein, Israel and Neil Asher Silberman. *The Bible Unearthed: Archaeology's New Vision of Ancient Israel and the Origin of Its Sacred Texts*. New York: Simon & Schuster, 2002.

Freedman, David Noel, ed. *Anchor Bible Dictionary*. 6 vols. New York: Doubleday, 1992.

Garbini, Giovanni. *History and Ideology in Ancient Israel*. Translated by John Bowden. New York: Crossroad, 1988.

Gibson, J. C. L. *Language and Imagery in the Old Testament*. Peabody, MA: Hendrickson, 1998.

Gunkel, Hermann. *Genesis*. Macon, GA: Mercer University Press, 1997.

Harris, Stephen L. *Understanding the Bible*, 6th ed. Boston: McGraw-Hill, 2003.

Huesman, John E. "Exodus." *The Jerome Biblical Commentary* (1968): 50–51 (OT).

Josephus, Flavius. *The Complete Works of Josephus*. Translated by W. Whiston. Grand Rapids, MI: Kregel, 1981.

Karris, Robert J., ed. *The Collegeville Bible Commentary*. Collegeville, MN: Liturgical Press, 1988.

Keller, Werner. *The Bible as History*. New York: William Morrow and Co., 1981.

Kensky, Tikva Frymer. *Reading the Women of the Bible: A New Interpretation of Their Stories*. New York: Shocken Books, 2002.

Kugel, James L. *The Bible as It Was*. Cambridge, MA: Belknap Press, 1997.

Lemche, Niels Peter. *Prelude to Israel's Past: Background and Beginnings of Israelite History and Identity*. Translated by E. F. Maniscalco. Peabody, MA: Hendrickson, 1998.

Meyers, Carol. "Contesting the Notion of Patriarchy: Anthropology and the Theorizing of Gender in Ancient Israel." Pp. 84–105 in *A Question of Sex? Gender and Difference in the Hebrew Bible* (Hebrew Bible monographs, 14), ed. Deborah Rooke. Sheffield UK: Sheffield Phoenix Press, 2007.

Meyers, Carol, Toni Craven, and Ross S. Kraemer, eds. *Women in Scripture: A Dictionary of Named and Unnamed Women in the Hebrew Bible, The Apocryphal/Deuterocanonical Books, and The New Testament*. New York: Houghton Mifflin Co., 2000.

Milgrom, Jacob. "Numbers." *JPS Torah Commentary*. Philadelphia: JPS, 1990.

Mobley, Gregory, "The Wild Man in the Bible and the Ancient Near East." *Journal of Biblical Literature* 116 (1997): 217–233.

Moriarty, Frederick L. "Numbers." *The Jerome Biblical Commentary* (1968): 95 (OT).

Nielsen, Kirsten. *Ruth: A Commentary*. Translated by E. Broadbridge. *Old Testament Library*. Louisville: Westminster/John Knox Press, 1997.

Newsom, Carol A. and Sharon H. Ringe, eds. *The Women's Bible Commentary*. Louisville: Westminster/John Knox, 1992.

Pritchard, James B. *Ancient Near Eastern Texts Relating to the Old Testament*. 3rd ed. Princeton, NJ: Princeton University Press, 1969.

von Rad, Gerhard. *The Message of the Prophets*. San Francisco: Harper Collins, 1967.

Schulz, Regine and Matthias Seidel, eds. *Egypt: The World of the Pharaohs*. Köln: Könemann, 2002.

Senior, Donald and John J. Collins, eds. *The Catholic Study Bible: New American Bible*. 2nd edition. New York: Oxford University Press, 2006.

Smelik, Klaas A. D. *Writings from Ancient Israel: A Handbook of Historical and Religious Documents*. Louisville: Westminster/John Knox, 1991.

Smith, Mark. *The Early History of God: Yahweh and the Other Deities in Ancient Israel*. 2nd ed. Grand Rapids, MI: Eerdmans, 2002.

Speiser, E. A. *The Anchor Bible: Genesis*. New York: Doubleday & Co., Inc., 1964.

Steinberg, Naomi A. *Kinship and Marriage in Genesis: A Household Economics Perspective*. Minneapolis: Fortress Press, 1993.

Yee, Gale A., ed. *Judges and Method: New Approaches in Biblical Studies*. Minneapolis: Fortress Press, 1995.

Recommended Reading

Belis, Alice Ogden. *Helpmates, Harlots, and Heroes: Women's Stories in the Hebrew Bible*. Louisville: Westminster/John Knox Press, 1994.

Deen, Edith. *All the Women of the Bible*. New York: Harper Collins, 1988.

Demers, Patricia. *Women as Interpreters of the Bible*. New York: Paulist Press, 1992.

Kensky, Tikva Frymer. *Reading the Women of the Bible: A New Interpretation of Their Stories*. New York: Shocken Books, 2002.

Meyers, Carol. "Contesting the Notion of Patriarchy: Anthropology and the Theorizing of Gender in Ancient Israel." Pp. 84–105 in *A Question of Sex? Gender and Difference in the Hebrew Bible* (Hebrew Bible monographs, 14), ed. Deborah Rooke. Sheffield UK: Sheffield Phoenix Press, 2007

Meyers, Carol, Toni Craven and Ross S. Kraemer, eds. *Women in Scripture: A Dictionary of Named and Unnamed Women in the Hebrew Bible, The Apocryphal/Deuterocanonical Books, and The New Testament*. New York: Houghton Mifflin Co., 2000.

Newsom, Carol A. and Sharon H. Ringe, eds. *The Women's Bible Commentary*. Louisville: Westminster/John Knox, 1992.

Index